Only You

Only You

The Unexpected Gift of Being Alone

DR MARNY LISHMAN

WILEY

A catalogue record for this book is available from the National Library of Australia

Registered Office
John Wiley & Sons Australia, Ltd. Level 4, 600 Bourke Street, Melbourne, VIC 3000, Australia

For details of our global editorial offices, customer services, and more information about Wiley products visit us at www.wiley.com.

Wiley also publishes its books in a variety of electronic formats and by print-on-demand. Some content that appears in standard print versions of this book may not be available in other formats.

Cover design by Wiley
Cover image: © Tatiana Magurova/Getty Images
Author Photo: Donna Fortune Photography

Set in 11/16 pts and Palatino LT Std by Straive, Chennai, India.

SKYEA6F1985-85CA-4843-8E8C-8D16DEC37AD7_040226

This is for anyone who, for whatever reason,
finds themselves alone.

xx

Contents

Introduction

INT. BAR — SUNSET

Marny and a friend sit by the window at a popular wine bar overlooking the beach. They sip from glasses of prosecco, people-watching as they gossip.

MARNY

Jeffrey Dean Morgan.

FRIEND

Who?

MARNY

You know, Jeffrey Dean Morgan. He was that Denny guy in *Grey's Anatomy* who needed the heart transplant. I think he's in *The Walking Dead*. And that *P.S. I Love You* movie. The hot one. Like he is super-hot.

FRIEND

Oh yeah, I err … maybe?

Marny's friend rolls her eyes upwards and to the left, as if she is searching her mind back to her early twenties when she watched Grey's Anatomy.

MARNY

Okay, well I'm sending you a photo.

Marny pulls out her phone and Googles Jeffrey Dean Morgan one-handed, looking for an image of her celebrity crush. She juggles her glass of prosecco in the other hand as she airdrops a photo to her friend.

Ooooh here's a better one. This one has three Jeffrey Dean Morgans on it, and there are three age choices — you've got one in his thirties, one in his forties and then an older one. Like one from what he looks like now. So, Jeffrey at any age is good.

FRIEND

Okay, yeah rightio. I actually don't think I've ever seen a man that looks like that in real life. But anyways …

MARNY

So, if the next guy you try and set me up with doesn't look like one of these Jeffrey Dean Morgan photos … don't bother.

Marny sips her prosecco, only half-joking.

These types of exchanges with my friends are not uncommon. They send me suggestions of single men they know or show me photos of someone they think would be perfect. Then I reply with some lame excuse. My excuses have been quite ridiculous, really, when you think about them. Too short. Too rich. Too full-on. Too nice. Too clingy. Too daggy. Too feminine. Too old. Too bogan. Too much of a 'player'.

'He talks way too much', I said to a friend once, who has since been on the hunt for a handsome mute for me.

Given what you've just read, you won't be too surprised to hear that I've been single for quite some time. After a couple of long-term relationships and a few 'situationships' peppered with some dates here and there, I've nicely settled into being by myself. And I've been by myself for many years. Like ... for *many* years. So naturally, in every conversation I have with my friends about romance (or the lack thereof), they are tempted to try and lure me back into dating, with me either whippet-like replying, 'Is he better than my solitude?' or embarking on a lengthy description of an out-of-reach celebrity prototype of what they need to be looking for if they *do* bravely choose to set me up with someone (that's where Jeffrey Dean Morgan comes in—*what a handsome man*).

Don't get me wrong: I think dating is a wonderful way to get to know people if you want to find a relationship. I just don't want to do it. The thought of spending time with people I don't know (yet) really isn't that enticing to me.

At the moment, anyway.

I don't even have any dating horror stories to share. If I flick through the dating catalogue in my mind, all my dates have been decent experiences with nice men. But those guys will be more fitting for someone else, not me. Well, there was that one guy who was the second coming of 'Crocodile' Dundee...but there was nothing wrong with him or the dating experience, it's just that winklepickers and reptile teeth accessories are not my style.

My closest friends ceased trying to set me up with guys or even to suggest anyone a long time ago. Some friends even know me so well that if someone else says to them, 'Oh, he might be nice for Marny', they automatically say no on my behalf. They reject by proxy. I don't even realise that I've rejected anyone until months or even years later, when their name pops up in conversation. My friends know that people shouldn't even bother trying with me. They've tried and they've failed, and they don't want to put others through the same frustration when I inevitably knock back another reasonable man.

The problem here does not lie with the perfectly acceptable men (which I'm sure they would have been, if I'd given them half a chance) I've been set up with. It lies with me, as I continue to come up with ninja-like excuses to avoid bringing a man into my life on a permanent basis. I enjoy being alone, and it's been so long since I've been in a long-term relationship that I am very much used to it. I am content, despite how odd it may seem to others. I rarely feel lonely, and if this feeling does arise, albeit briefly, I have plenty of healthy strategies to ensure it disappears in a reasonable amount of time.

Contentment in being alone. Who would have thought it? Who knew it could be done?

Whether you're alone for two days, two weeks, two months, two years or two decades, many people find being alone challenging. Time and time again, as a therapist, I've listened to people who are clearly distressed during time spent alone. The space, gap, interim, window, period—whatever you want to call it, this time is often perceived as being in limbo. It's like a no man's land (pardon the pun) of time, in between what was and what's next. And sadly, so many people are treating this time as if nothing can be grown during it.

Being by themselves, particularly when they're not used to it, can considerably impact a person's wellbeing. More so if they are navigating loss or heartbreak (or both) on top of it. And because of the hot pot of emotions that may have been created and stirred by the whole experience that led to them being alone, they move far too quickly out of the uncomfortableness of it all, pouring themselves into another person to fill the void. Too many people jump out of the stillness, unease and silence that can come, at first, with being alone, and they miss out on the valuable transformation that can happen in this temporary state of discomfort. Too many people are searching for happiness, security, safety and comfort with someone new, but they are doing it far too quickly, all the while neglecting to create those feelings for themselves first. Too many people are not processing their emotions or reflecting on their learnings, but nor are they spending time finding out who they really are, which means they miss out on discovering the wisdom within them that can often lead to a richer, more fulfilling life.

This happens through no fault of the people I work with. We've all been there. I've been there too: upset, sad and even distraught that I'm not part of a couple, and unhelpfully comparing my imperfect single status to everyone else's seemingly perfect coupledom. Making the mistake of believing everyone who is in a relationship is happy and, of course, has it all (well, their social media account says it, so it must be true—#couplegoals #truelove #myforever #soulmates #wanderlust).

The unsolicited advice from well-meaning, coupled-up friends doesn't help either, as they tell us in our perceived single misery that we need to 'get back out there', 'give him a chance' and 'get back on the market'. In modern society, there's an unhelpful paradigm that most of us have grown up with—one that says being single is something we must fix, and if we are not locked in arms with a partner then we should at least be on the hunt for one. This paradigm suggests that if we're sans partner, we are likely living through an unfulfilling waiting period until we get back into a relationship.

All of us will likely be alone at some point, either by choice or because it has been imposed on us. Sometimes *aloneness* is for a moment, sometimes it's for a while and sometimes it feels like forever. Sometimes aloneness is craved, but it is mostly feared — likely because it is symbiotically and unhelpfully tied to *loneliness*. We've learned that the two go hand in hand.

But being alone doesn't equate to feeling lonely, in the same way that not being alone doesn't equate to not feeling lonely. Being in a relationship with someone doesn't always guarantee you won't feel disconnected, disengaged or just psychologically on a different page from your partner. Many of us have been there. We can be in a relationship and feel lonely even if there is someone lying beside us in our bed. Many people are there now.

So, seeing as we will all have a moment or two of being alone on our life journey, surely knowing how to do alone well will be useful. Instead of nose diving into the depths of psychological distress when it happens, we can learn to push past the initial discomfort and discover a different way to live that can be beneficial in so many ways.

Being alone is not something that should be feared; in fact, it might be just the thing you need. Whatever the reason behind you being alone is, and however distressing it may have been, it is so helpful to realise that being alone can be the catalyst for massive personal growth and a reset that leads to a better life ahead. Understanding the benefits of being alone is what this book is all about. As a therapist and self-proclaimed single and not-quite-ready-to-mingle, I feel I have some personal and professional expertise to guide you here. I'm not in any rush, so nor should you be!

But...loneliness is not a good thing, I hear you say? Yes, I agree with you. As a mental health professional who peddles the importance of connection, I know all about the negative effects of loneliness and will always urge people to 'be' with others—to make sure they are connected with their fellow human beings in some way. This book isn't about avoiding people. It's about the surprising psychological benefits of spending time alone (as in, not in a relationship) and utilising that time to reconnect with the people around you and, more importantly, yourself. It's a 'how to do alone well' guide, whether you're alone for a few days, a couple of weeks, many months or for years. It can even help if you plan to be 'alone' for eternity.

Throughout this book, I've drawn from my real-life experiences as a single person (and a coupled-up person), as well as drawn on some of my client experiences as a therapist. Every client I discuss is anonymised, and the examples from my life…well, they are all me!

I'm gathering that you've picked up this book because you, yourself, have been alone lately and may be feeling lonely. Or maybe you haven't been alone at all, yet you are feeling lonely anyway. Maybe you are not alone and you're not feeling lonely at all, but you feel that being alone for a while would be good for you (quick answer—it probably will). Maybe it's for none of those reasons and you just want to learn more about yourself. Hell, maybe you just loved the look of the book cover on the shelf (understandable!). Whatever the reason that has led you to this book, I'm sure you will benefit from what I've got to say in these pages. I'm sure your life going forward will be physically, mentally, emotionally and spiritually richer for spending some hours here with me.

I have split this book up into three distinct parts. **Part I** is all about how *being alone doesn't have to be lonely*. Mental health professionals like using terms such as 'holding space', and that is what I aim to do in these early pages. Holding space means to be present with how you are feeling right now, whatever those feelings may be.

Given that you've picked up this book, you may be feeling a little lonely or even lost. I want to sit in this feeling with you and make space for it in these early pages, without interfering with it too much. I will talk with you about how challenging loneliness can be for people, and how being alone, however difficult at first, can be life changing—in a good way. We'll discuss why we feel lonely, how people become alone, and how we can be lonely but not alone (yes, we can feel lonely even when we're surrounded by people). In addition to acknowledging these challenges, I will light a spark in you to let you know about the magic that can happen with a bit of solitude—so don't push your time alone away too quickly!

Part II takes us *from heartbreak to healing* and is where I will outline a few additional steps that we might need to take before we become comfortable with being alone. Sometimes we need to heal from certain life challenges and the experiences that led to us being alone. Often, we don't become 'alone' by choice (at the beginning, anyway). Some of the emotions and thoughts we may still be grasping on to could be keeping us stuck, making us feel we don't want to hang out for too long in our own company. We'll talk about the messiness of heartbreak, sitting with your feelings, healing after goodbye, claiming your emotional baggage and tapping into your wisdom (yes, you are a lot wiser than you may realise!). I will get you to reflect a little after each of these chapters.

Part III is all about getting comfortable with *being only you* and tapping into who you truly are. We will talk a lot about you becoming the best version of yourself, whether that means staying alone for just a little bit—or a while! I will highlight some of the areas that I've covered with my own clients over the years to get them to move from loneliness to contentment with being alone, including learning to relish in your presence, follow your inner compass, master your mind, listen to your emotions, own your inner strength, tap into your creativity and nurture your relationships (yes, you may be alone but you can still be connected — you're not getting away with not being around people!). I also get you thinking about how some self-compassion wouldn't go astray when you're feeling lonely and why tapping into your loneliness can help you develop your true self. Then we talk about those who are a little more fed up with being by themselves, deeming it far too long that they've been alone and, of course, those people who are not alone, nor lonely, that I believe could benefit from a little more 'alone time'. At the end of each chapter in Part III I ask you to reflect on your own experience and take charge with an *Only You* 'Motto' you may find helpful. I also 'Challenge' you with an activity that may help move you towards feeling content with being alone. You're not escaping from this without a little bit of work!

And then, just in case you haven't learned enough tips and tricks throughout (or you just blatantly forgot), I share a '101 Lovely Things to Do When You're Alone' cheat sheet you can refer to forevermore. In fleeting (or slightly longer) moments of loneliness, you can flick to the back of this book, close your eyes, twirl your finger around and point to a random activity to try out.

Finally, I present you with my *Only You* 'Monthly Review', which gives you the chance to wrap up everything you have learned throughout the book and focus on what you specifically want to work on each month to move away from loneliness, relish in the benefits of being alone and nurture yourself so you can be the best version of yourself.

As well as nourishing your own needs in life (apart from finding love), trying to be the best version of yourself gives you the opportunity to find (and even retain) your true self, something that many of us don't think to do when we're in a partnership. Valuing yourself (rather than trying to add value to your life through another person) is psychologically healthy, and being alone for a while can give you time to develop your relationship with yourself. All of us will be alone at some point in our lives, whether we like it or not. Understanding that you're so much more than one half of a couple is imperative to your life journey. It's so important to realise that you exist beyond being someone's partner.

In a world where people seem to rush too quickly to find themselves through other people, it's often when you're alone that you truly discover who you really are. This book is for those with broken hearts, who can't stand silence, who need people more than air, who feel abandoned, who feel contempt for their significant other, who've been dumped, who are serial swipers, who are grieving, who want to break-up but are too scared, who find being by themselves nearly impossible and for those who want to learn how to personally grow.

After reading this book, I want your alone time to evolve into time that is so interesting, relished, fun and nourishing that you never fear it again. I want you to get to know yourself so well that you really think hard about who and what you let in to the content life you've created. I've written this to disrupt the negative rhetoric about being alone—to tell you that it's nothing to fear but, rather, something to embrace. I urge you to be optimistic and push through the discomfort and find meaning in your solitude, whether it's for a short time or a little longer. I want the disconnection you may feel in loneliness to lead you on a pathway towards connecting more with your true self going forward.

Hey, you might want to hang out with yourself even more after reading this.

Part I

Being Alone Doesn't Have to Be Lonely

Chapter 1
Feeling Lonely

If you stop for a moment and think of the most beautiful songs composed in the past century, you will realise that they are rarely written with optimistic lyrics, filled with cheerful melodies, bouncing with peppy beats or sung with elated emotional gusto. Whether it's Sinéad O'Connor breathlessly telling someone after seven hours and 15 days of separation that 'Nothing Compares 2 U' or Eric Carmen singing how he doesn't want to be 'All by Myself', the songs are written as a calling of sorts, from people who are, now, all by themselves. Artists who we have never met validate exactly how we are feeling, or may have felt, at some point in our lives. We all know what song to dig out of the playlist when we need some validation for our own loneliness, to help us process the mess of heartbreak and to motivate us to get up and get on with our life alone. I've wallowed my way through more than a few Phil Collins songs in my time ... or perhaps it wasn't too many, but rather just enough.

Usually, these powerful songs are the ones that vibrate our chests, bring tears to our eyes, send tingles up our spine and force our hairs to stand on end, all the while managing to align with something inside of us—maybe a distant memory or a feeling we are experiencing in the present moment. These songs convey emotions of heartbreak, loss, unrequited love and, of course, loneliness. For many adults listening to these types of songs, whether on a crisp record, CD or favourite playlist, they have a resonance that is universal and familiar, along with their proverbial tugging at the heartstrings. These songs are the ones that we intentionally play to not only soothe ourselves in times of struggle, but to reassure ourselves that someone, somewhere, 'gets' the emotional pain we are feeling. Lyrics, music and melodies depict the forlorn nature of our disconnection from someone who meant something to us, our longing to get them back or the unbearable void left in their absence.

The Oxford Dictionary defines loneliness as 'sadness because one has no friends or company', while the Cambridge Dictionary sums the feeling up as 'unhappy because you are not with other people'. It's an emotion that can encompass a multitude of feelings, including sadness, emptiness, longing, isolation and not belonging, with the overarching theme of being unhappy or dissatisfied about not being with other people. However, it is also a subjective feeling too, with many people feeling lonely even while they are around people because they are not connecting with them. Anyone who exists daily amongst people and still feels 'othered' will know what I'm talking about here.

Essentially, loneliness involves people (being there or not) and *not feeling connected.*

The myriad emotions we feel in the modern world all serve a purpose. The emotion of loneliness is essential. Our lonely *Homo sapiens* ancestors would have felt extremely uncomfortable in the emotional pain of becoming lost from or even kicked out of their group. Without the safety, security and strength of being in a group, wandering around alone in the harsh wilderness would have made them a likely target for threats in their environment. Their brains would have sent chemical messengers in the form of emotions to alert them that they were alone in a harsh environment and more vulnerable to predators. A feeling of loneliness creeping over them would have led them to take certain actions to feel safe again (such as reconnecting to their group), which would have been crucial for survival.

Fast forward some 10 000 years or so, and many of us no longer have wild animals stalking us for their dinner, so we tend to marinate in some of our more negative-but-necessary emotions for far too long. If we're not driven by the innate need to act to survive, we may not only ignore some of these important emotions, but we might also use rather unhelpful coping mechanisms to numb them.

$$\bullet\ \bullet\ \bullet$$

'I'm just so lonely'.

This is what my client Melissa said to me one session, cross-legged on the couch in my office, hugging a blue cushion. We had just had a lengthy conversation about what she'd been doing in the past couple of months since she'd separated from her husband. As it was quite early in the initial stages of separation, Melissa was finding the quiet evenings without him in the house almost unbearable. Coming from a large family growing up and then going straight into a relationship upon moving out when she was 18, Melissa had never really spent time totally alone. Not only was it an unfamiliar feeling, but it was also uncomfortable, and she was not prepared to sit with the loneliness for too long. She worked all day with people, which was a suitable distraction that in many ways gave her a reprieve from intruding thoughts about her ex-husband and the associated angst. She also had two little children, which provided another diversion and added plenty of things for her to do at either ends of the day. But in the evenings, when she'd read the kids their bedtime stories, tuck them into their beds and wander back into her empty lounge, she just couldn't bear it. Quick to fill the silence, she would reach for a glass of wine and her phone, then talk for hours to different men through a dating app. This was quite uncharacteristic behaviour for her, but she was doing this because she knew she felt lonely. The emotional pain of not having her husband around anymore was something she wasn't prepared to wade in.

Some people, like Melissa, can feel the loneliness and articulate what it is, or at least notice that their behaviour is likely to be a result of feeling lonely. These people *feel* lonely, so they try to do something to shift it. But not everyone is like Melissa. Many people are not even aware of their feelings or, even if they are, they are not curious about them. They just feel lonely, then behave in what may be an uncharacteristic way, without too much self-inquiry between their feelings and their behaviours.

We have all done this with some of our 'uncomfortable' emotions:

> ➤ Feeling angry in the moment and then saying something stupid (and regretful) to a loved one
> ➤ Feeling shame about making a mistake, so spluttering out a lie to cover it up
> ➤ Feeling frustrated at work because of the unrealistic demands placed upon us, and then just quitting
> ➤ Feeling anxious about going to a social event, so we send a 'sorry, something's come up' message at the last minute
> ➤ Feeling lonely and then talking for hours to different men.

All these behaviours, which might not be problematic in themselves (although some might be), are usually not thoughtful responses but rather are emotionally driven—driven by the feeling, rather than a well thought out…thought. Reacting, rather than responding. Beneficial in the short term, but maybe not so beneficial in the long term. These automatic behaviours may ease the emotional pain at first, but they won't be as helpful as an action with more positive long-term outcomes — the kind we'd take if we'd only given ourselves some more time to think things through.

Being emotionally driven is something many of us do. But there's a quiet, almost insidious mechanism at play with loneliness. Unlike anger, which can literally hit you in the face, loneliness can just creep up silently and then simmer away, causing you to become someone entirely different to who you were before. You're not really bothering people with your loneliness, so it can stay longer and is often unnoticed by others, even ourselves. Many people have likely been feeling lonely for a while and have unwittingly been covering it up.

People almost become defensive about their disconnection, not realising that the likely reason their psychological wellbeing has gone awry is because they are lonely. When visiting a psychologist, therapist or counsellor, the presenting problem might be something else and then, after a bit of digging and disclosing, it becomes clear that the root problem lies in escaping the loneliness. If I think about my clients over the past few decades, it's easy to reflect on the number of people whose irrational thoughts, out-of-character behaviours and uncomfortable feelings were driven by loneliness, even if they were not aware of it at the time, such as ending a relationship on a Wednesday and being out dating again on a Thursday, life-hacking their way through the loneliness as soon as they possibly can. After both of my long-term relationship breakups, I pretty much skipped the loneliness part, almost like a predictive text that presumed what I needed next, busying myself with bar-hopping with friends and, of course, dating. I moved past the silence and the unknown I unconsciously knew would be there if I stopped. And I'm certainly not alone in doing this.

So, lonely doesn't always mean 'feeling lonely'. Loneliness presents differently in different people. Sadness, emptiness and feeling unseen are common descriptors. But people also unintentionally mask these uncomfortable feelings with certain behaviours that may not be ideal for them. It might be one too many wines in the evening, endlessly talking to people online, hours of gaming in one's bedroom, or staying in bed and sleeping way too much. It might be binge-watching TV, too many Tinder dates, constantly scrolling through social media, staying with the wrong person for way too long, seeking validation through likes and comments on posts, working overtime to keep busy, or even making impulsive purchases or developing negative habits. I once had a client that was talking to a Hollywood TV star online and transferred them $5000, likely because they were so lonely (unfortunately, the person was not a Hollywood TV star, go figure). Each of these behaviours serves as a temporary distraction or disguise, helping individuals momentarily escape feelings of loneliness or emotional emptiness.

Many behaviours that can become addictive vices are caused by loneliness. Journalist and author Johann Hari, in his book *Lost Connections*, goes as far as to say, 'The opposite of addiction is not sobriety. It is human connection'. And I would dare to agree.

Loneliness can feel painful. It's kind of supposed to feel like this. At first, anyway. If our ancestors didn't feel this emotional pain, they could easily have become separated from their pack and been eaten by a sabre-toothed tiger because they didn't get the 'lonely' memo to warn them. Those who felt lonely were propelled to get back to their people, quick smart! This is a reductionist example, of course, but loneliness, like all our emotions, served a purpose for our survival.

The thing about our emotions in the past is that when we felt them, we would have been driven by the feeling and 'acted' to survive.

In modern times, we don't do this so much. We might feel these emotions and then, instead of inquiring about the feeling or even using the valuable information they are giving us, we either don't notice the feeling (because we are so caught up in other things and not that self-aware), ignore them, blunt them, unhelpfully soothe them, or just do absolutely nothing and stew miserably in them (sometimes for years). We don't use those emotions to think about what the best thing to do might be—the thing or things that we really need to do to make our lives sustainably better.

As author Oscar Wilde said in his novel, *The Picture of Dorian Gray*: 'I don't want to be at the mercy of my emotions. I want to use them, to enjoy them, and to dominate them'. Let's all start to do this a little more when we start feeling lonely. Let's not skip it. Let's feel the emotion and listen to what it is whispering to us.

Chapter 2

The Trouble with Loneliness

In early 2020, Australians were glued to their screens, watching as global COVID-19 cases, and deaths, climbed by the hour. Most of us had never experienced anything like it. We waited anxiously for our state leaders to announce whether we should stay at home, wear masks, send our kids to school or show up to work, all while confronting harrowing images from overwhelmed hospitals overseas and wondering if it was a sign of what was to come for us. Those first few months of that year were chaotic. With uncertainty dragging on and guidance changing every day, stress and anxiety spread rapidly. The chaos wasn't just external—it was seeping into our homes, our workplaces, our relationships and our minds. For us psychologists it was business as usual, but we found ourselves busier than ever, helping people navigate a parallel pandemic of stress, anxiety and emotional overload. Existing mental health struggles were amplified and, beneath it all, we could feel something deeper brewing. We weren't just dealing with a killer virus; we were heading into the biggest mental health crisis of our lifetime, and we're still dealing with the after-effects of it all.

Before the pandemic, virtual meetings were already part of how we communicated, but during the pandemic, they became crucial. In-person contact wasn't just discouraged for many businesses — it was banned under strict lockdowns across the country. Where I live in Perth, Western Australia, we were relatively unscathed compared to other regions, but I noticed a marked difference in the people I was working with during that first year, especially those from the eastern states and overseas who dealt with harsher circumstances. Alongside running virtual professional development seminars, where I beamed into makeshift home offices to teach strategies for managing stress, adapting to disruption and coping with uncertainty, I was also conducting virtual psychological consults. These sessions offered a deeper insight into the emotional toll of the pandemic. I heard story after story about people separated from their families overseas, unable to travel even in emergencies. Some were stuck in different cities from their partners or children, facing indefinite separation. Others were completely alone, trapped within four walls, with no end in sight and nothing to meaningfully distract them from the weight of isolation. With loneliness creeping in and nothing but more screens to buffer it, many people were suffering. They were stressed, scared, fearful, uncertain, anxious and exhausted. One of my clients at the time likened himself to a houseplant that hadn't had enough light and water — a little dull and lifeless.

What I remember most clearly from that time was the energy coming through the screens of my clients, as well as the energy from the professionals listening to my seminars in their temporary work setups in their homes. Despite my efforts to bring connection, support and encouragement into those virtual rooms, I could feel the disconnection, the lethargy and a kind of quiet despair. Being alone for lengthy periods and not doing anything healthy with that time contributed to the loneliness people were feeling. Now and again, you would find a jolly soul who was basking in being alone and having a good time (likely the introverts among us) but, for the most part, people were struggling. It was as if people's spirits were slowly fading, their souls withering from prolonged solitude and the sheer emotional exhaustion of not knowing when, or if, life would return to normal. Loneliness was brewing, marinating and simmering for far too long.

A feeling is an extension of emotion. Emotions are chemical messengers that tell us about what is working and not working for us in our environment (internally and externally), and they are supposed to propel us to move in a particular direction that would enable us to be in a better state. These messengers are giving us important information, particularly when something in our context needs adjustment because it's undermining our wellbeing. Loneliness is an uncomfortable feeling, and there is a sense of unease that comes over us when we're experiencing it. It's a universal feeling that everyone can experience. Fearing rejection, fearing judgement and fearing failure is also wired into us because being disconnected from our group could lead to us dying prematurely from a looming threat in the environment. That's why we find it hard to take risks, we feel bad when we do something stupid, and we beat ourselves up when we stuff up. The most uncomfortable and distressing emotions we feel today would have helped our ancestors to survive, and the loneliness emotion would be included in that repertoire. But too much of anything is a bad thing — while momentary loneliness is crucial for human survival, lingering loneliness is not good for our wellbeing. Like all our emotions, loneliness isn't supposed to stay unnoticed and unactioned long term, and if it does it has the potential to cause us quite a few problems.

In recent years, particularly post-pandemic, loneliness has become one of the most discussed psychological issues of our time, with proclamations of 'a loneliness epidemic' in hundreds of media headlines across the globe. According to the World Health Organization's (WHO) 2025 report, *From Loneliness to Social Connection: Charting a Path to Healthier Societies*, worldwide loneliness affects about 1 in 6 people (16 per cent), with certain groups more susceptible than others. People in low-income countries and young people are particularly at risk, while populations experiencing marginalisation are also likely to experience social disconnection. The WHO has declared loneliness to be a public health issue.

Researchers are also uncovering just how deeply loneliness can shape our minds, bodies and behaviours. Psychologically, it has been shown to contribute to and exacerbate other health conditions that one might already be suffering from, such as depression and anxiety. Goodness knows that anxiety loves spare time. The space that is created by an initial disconnection from those around us is a twilight zone of nothingness; if you don't fill it with something, your anxiety will fill it with unhelpful thoughts, like worries about the future and ruminations about the past. Such worries can unhelpfully entertain us for hours, like a ticker-tape parade of everything that can go wrong or has gone wrong—rendering us even more likely to be distressed and to choose to disconnect from the world.

Chronic loneliness can also shape our personalities over time. Not only does loneliness feel uncomfortable, disconnecting and miserable, but it also brings to bear unique effects on personality beyond this that may flow on to other areas of your life—losing your mojo to exercise, eat well or take risks on your dreams. It's almost an out-of-awareness realisation that makes you wonder if something is worth doing at all if you're not doing it for or with others—a 'what's the point of doing this?' feeling that's demotivating, to say the least. These results would likely resonate with anyone who has more negative memories of spending time alone, reflecting on how out of character they may have been behaving during that period—skipping their workouts, ordering food in way too much or not being as productive as they usually are.

Another line of research has shown that loneliness affects not just how we see others but also how we view ourselves. A study by Kent *et al*, published in 2025 in the journal *Psychophysiology*, found that lonely people have more negative self-perceptions and were more likely to believe they offered less support and created more strain in their relationships. Lingering loneliness often has a way of turning us inwards in an unhealthy way—homing in on our perceived flaws, causing us to be more critical of ourselves, and rendering us more anxious and more depressed. Loneliness also appears to impact the stability of other emotions. The results of a study that tracked the emotional lives of adults by Lazuras, Ypsilanti and Mullings, published in 2024 in the *International Journal of Behavioural Medicine*, showed that people who reported higher levels of loneliness experienced more emotional volatility, especially in their positive emotions (which may otherwise have helpfully balanced out any negative emotions). The lonelier people feel, the more they struggle to sustain good feelings, which could contribute to poorer health over time.

The impact of loneliness on physical health has not gone unnoticed. A groundbreaking study by Shen *et al*, reported in *Nature Human Behaviour* in 2025, found that loneliness and social isolation are associated with biological changes that may increase disease risk. They found that lonely individuals had elevated levels of specific proteins linking to inflammation, immune function and brain health.

Loneliness is a universally felt emotion that all of us will likely feel at some stage in our lives. However adaptive and useful the emotion was to our ancestors, many of us don't particularly like feeling it; it's perceived in quite a negative light, and it's rather unhealthy. We will all likely be alone at some point in our lives and loneliness may come along with it, so it will pay in so many ways for us to learn to do it better.

As Janet Fitch said in her novel *White Oleander*: 'Loneliness is the human condition. Cultivate it. The way it tunnels into you allows your soul room to grow'.

So, let's start growing.

Chapter 3

Becoming Alone

Sometimes I feel that I was destined to be alone.

Now, a bit of a disclaimer: I spend a considerable amount of time with people throughout the day—almost too much, my introverted self would argue—so I'm not completely alone. I have family and friends who I spend a lot of time with, pets that follow me everywhere, kids that talk (a lot) and, professionally, my job literally involves other people. So, when I'm talking about feeling destined to be alone, I don't mean *alone* alone but, you know, *not in a relationship* alone.

I also feel like somewhat of an anomaly in that in recent years, in my current 'middle age' stage of life, I've put zero effort into finding a partner. Maybe even negative effort, if that's possible, in that I reject people—perfectly fine people—before I've given any thought to whether they would be a good match for me. I say 'thank you but no thank you' at ninja-like speed to someone who asks me out. I just cut off the idea as quick as the next person at the supermarket checkout does when they slam the divider down to separate their shopping from yours. They don't want your baked beans touching their spaghetti. It's nothing personal; they just don't have the time for anything deeper in the present moment, so they take their shopping and walk away. Alas, this is me.

I don't meet many people who think like this. I meet a lot of people who wouldn't mind being alone for a while; I have friends who say that if they were without their partner (for some godforsaken reason), they would be okay by themselves—but when this actually happens, they don't cope as well as they'd predicted. Instead, they desperately try to escape being 'alone' before 'lonely' enters the door, quickly pairing up with someone new and returning their Facebook status to 'in a relationship'.

From an evolutionary perspective, we are wired to be with other people. Many of us have an almost unconscious urge to hook up with people the moment we are biologically ready, and we rarely stop to think anything different. We default to pairing up or quickly searching for a special person to embark on a relationship with when we are by ourselves longer than we deem to be normal. When people are by themselves for a while, other people tend to wonder *why*. It seems more socially acceptable to stay in an unhealthy or even downright rotten relationship than to not be in one at all. It's seen as more normal to go on endless dates and endure small talk and awkward silences than it is to enjoy your own company and stay at home in your fluffy bunny slippers while doing more interesting activities. Or maybe that's just me.

Perhaps I'm a rarity for thinking that being alone is good. Is there something wrong with me? Even though I feel content with being alone, I sometimes wonder if I should feel differently. I occasionally slip into thinking I should be putting more effort into finding a new relationship, and I shouldn't be so quick to reject people when I'm asked out—that I should, as many people have suggested, 'give him a chance'. I often feel bad that I may have hurt someone's feelings, but then I remember that it's society giving me this 'should' rule—it's not my rule. People are so quick to try and 'fix' people who are single, often to make themselves feel comfortable, that they encourage others to re-couple to fit in. But I'm wondering why people are not considering being alone more. Being alone can be transformative. I think many people would be very different to who they are now if they gave themselves some time to be alone. Time alone can be good for you, and it has been for me.

On the other hand, I don't intend to be single forever, and I'm certainly looking forward to the day I find my 'soul mate', my future 'partner' or 'my person' (who knows what I will refer to him as! It's been so long). 'One day, I'm going to walk into your house for a family dinner with an actual boyfriend, and you are all just going to *die*', I have exaggeratingly said to my family, who squint at me as if they don't believe this could ever happen after all these years of me arriving solo at family dinners.

But these are the family and friends who know, deep down, that I'm not so much being a fussy pain in the butt (which is also quite valid given some of the terrible reasons I have come up with to get out of a date) but carefully considering who I let into my life going forward. They know that the next guy I embark on a relationship with—this unicorn of a man that I will dismantle my brick wall for—needs to be an absolute bonus to my life. He needs to be better than my solitude. And I, hopefully, will be better than his. I am *only me* but I'm certainly not *lonely*, so I don't want to rush it—particularly when I have other things to do.

I've been without a partner for many years, and I have not put any effort into finding a new one. I'm an extremely busy solo mum, raising two kids by myself. Looking at my schedule in the hope of finding a skerrick of spare time, where I don't have my mum, daughter or business owner (oh, and writer) hat on, is near impossible, particularly when you really think hard about the multitude of tasks and duties that come off the back of all those roles. Never mind all the other pressures on my time, good and bad — finding the time to spend with my beautiful friends, staying fit, taking care of my parents, keeping my skin moisturised … we all have to manage our time as best we can. As a modern woman, even just scrolling through social media feels exhausting. Every post is a new mandate: lift heavier, wake up earlier, inject this, take that, eat this, don't eat that, look perfect, make this bigger, make that smaller, be successful, stay productive … but also make sure you go on regular trips to Europe to find yourself (please note, I do not have time for most of this). Honestly, the idea of going rogue, ditching it all, and living all hairy and off the grid like a contestant on the TV show *Alone* starts to sound like the ultimate act of self-care. I imagine it could be quite restful.

If you're a parent, you've also got to consider your kids and what is best for them if you're thinking of bringing someone new into your life. A few years ago, when my son was nine, he quietly warned (threatened) me that if I ever brought a guy home to become his stepfather, he would, and I quote, 'cut off his balls'. Luckily, this threat has since been lifted, so I'm free to date now if I choose — but only if I run my date choice by my son first (all balls will remain safely intact). So, understandably, I have been very mindful of bringing anyone home to meet the kiddies — one of the many, many reasons that I've personally chosen to remain alone for a long time.

I'm also an Aquarius (if you believe in all that) and embody all the astrological traits of an Aquarian: lives in their head, independent, eccentric and often deviates from the crowd to do their own thing. All me. I'm also an otrovert (more about that in Chapter 5), so being around people all the time is not a prerequisite for me to have a fulfilling day. Adding to this, I also have a nature-child archetype, meaning that I need to be immersed in nature and surrounded by animals to feel most alive. Sitting in the woods singing Snow

White-style to doe-eyed deer, cotton-tail bunnies and baby bluebirds would be an ideal social outing for me.

Let's also throw some spiritual 'woo-woo' into the mix. A few years ago, after a rather devastating relationship breakup that was extremely difficult to heal from (I'm not even sure if I'm there yet, to be honest), I proactively embarked on a healing journey that one would say was a little out of the norm—in the spirit realm, to look at it another way. As a mental health professional who is confidently grounded in many of the most effective mind and body techniques used to heal from adversity, I still felt I needed a little more, so I delved into the ancient wisdom that is ignored way too often in Western cultures. I learned about an advanced Aboriginal healing modality known as holographic kinetics, so I took it upon myself to find a local practitioner. While lying on a table in a strange little room attached to the practitioner's house, he started a curious hour-or-so-long process with me that involved looking into the internal, invisible dimensions of my life. I didn't really understand it too much at the time, but it meant tuning into my spirit in this lifetime as a young child, and then into several of my past lives. He asked me to describe with all my senses what I was experiencing in every one of those dimensions. After exploring the surroundings of each of the many lives that my spirit had lived (in this life and in past lives), my practitioner asked me to describe in detail the people I was surrounded with. My response each time?

'There's no one around me. I'm alone'.

Go figure.

We just need to throw in a few relationships that didn't work out in this lifetime, and boom—here I am again. Alone. So maybe the fact that I'm comfortable being alone is because of myriad reasons. All these weird and wonderful insights into myself, in this life (and past lives), seem to have led me to being alone right now. Hell, if my spirit has been by itself for hundreds of years, surely I've had enough time to get used to it.

But that's enough of my 'quirky alone' tales and the juicy non-existent details of all the dates I haven't gone on lately. Let's move on to the important stuff. Many of us have been alone before, and many of us will find ourselves alone at some point, and for a variety of reasons. People often talk about how awful it is to be alone, without a partner—whether it is for a short or a long period of time. Romance stories fill the shelves and dominate bestseller lists, yet no one really talks about the experience of being alone. In a world that glamourises love, lust and happily ever after, the bookshop feels noticeably empty when you're searching for guidance on what to do when the romance fades and the fairytales end. Statistically, many relationships don't work out. Sounds grim, but it's true. So, it's important to realise that you're not alone if you're alone.

One of the most common reasons people seek out a mental health professional is because of a relationship breakdown, whether it's a breakup, a divorce or the slow fading of a once-deep connection. Heartbreak can leave people reeling—not just from the loss of a partner, but from the sudden shift in identity and routine. They wonder, 'Who am I if I am not with this person?' It marks the beginning of an unfamiliar chapter, where individuals are left to navigate the terrain of singledom while often feeling unanchored and alone. This kind of aloneness, coming off the back of love lost, is one of the most painful and disorienting for people. Even for those who instigated the breakup, getting used to a new normal is terribly discombobulating. I've spent countless sessions with clients who know, deep down, that their relationship isn't right—that their connection is no longer there, or perhaps they'd never truly connected at all. They carry the heavy realisation that staying means self-betrayal, yet the thought of leaving feels overwhelmingly frightening. The familiarity, even in its dysfunction, feels safer than the uncertainty of what comes next. The known, however painful, often feels easier to bear than the unknown. And, on occasion, after deep reflection and hard emotional work—after that powerful 'a-ha' moment when they realise the relationship just isn't going to work—they leave our session ready to end it. But, in many cases, they return the following week still in the relationship, pulled back by hope, fear or habit. I've seen this time and time again, and it breaks my heart a little to watch it happen.

Sometimes, we find ourselves alone not by choice or conflict, but through the profound loss of a partner passing away. In these moments, aloneness is intertwined with grief. This kind of aloneness carries a unique weight—one that isn't just about not being without someone, but about mourning a life that was shared and then cut too short. Our neural pathways and our love are still there for someone who is no longer with us.

Aloneness may not come from heartbreak or loss at all, but simply from the way life unfolds. In today's transient world, we move often—chasing jobs, relationships and adventure—and as we do so, we leave behind the communities and connections that once anchored us. It's not always a dramatic ending that leads to solitude, but the quiet drift of distance and time. We don't stay long enough in one place to lay down roots and, without meaning to, we may find ourselves unmoored in unfamiliar places. It may take a while to realise we're living without the people who once made us feel known and connected—those people who know us well enough to connect us to other people who then add further value to our lives. And then there are the times we might crave going out and meeting people, but we can't. The strict regulations and lockdowns during the COVID-19 pandemic were enormous in terms of the psychological impact they had on people, trapping us in our homes alone for far longer than is healthy. Overt dating was pretty tricky during those times, but I heard that covert operations remained steadily intact (yes, I'm talking about affairs).

Another common reason people find themselves alone, which is something I've seen often in my private practice, is when people feel as if they don't fit in. When someone sees themselves as part of a minority, or 'othered', they can start to believe they're misunderstood or disliked (whether it's true or not), leading them to withdraw and isolate, whether they feel it is their gender, sexuality, ethnicity, culture or other perceived difference that causes them to feel outside of the crowd. Over time, this self-imposed separation only lengthens and deepens the pain they feel about being alone, unintentionally reinforcing the very distance they fear.

Sometimes we become alone because we just *feel* like disconnecting and being by ourselves for a while, directed by our emotions, which have thought it best that we withdraw from society for a bit—whether this is because of anxiety, depression, stress, burnout or a physical health condition. This choice can lead us to get used to being alone—and the longer we leave it, the harder it becomes to step back into being around people. Anyone who has felt the FOGO (Fear of Going Out) after being huddled away in their home for too long will recognise this fear.

Some even say that as we age, we all become more introverted. The introverts among us might open up for a while during their teenage years and young adulthood to meet people and procreate, before going back into their shells. But even the extroverts, who need people for their energy, may start slowing down as they age, preferring to retreat from society over time.

As a busy midlifer, one that is part of the sandwich generation, I yearn for more alone time. I want to step away from society a little bit more than I've ever done, so I can reset, recharge and rejuvenate to better cope with circumstances that sometimes place too many demands on me. If I'm not putting in much effort to find a partner now, I can only imagine how much harder it will become in the years ahead. With the world weighed down by crises, political turmoil and uncertainty, it's easy to feel exhausted and lose the motivation to invest in relationships. When you're already struggling to give life your all, those external pressures only make the whole process feel even more overwhelming and discouraging. You won't find me on Tinder anytime soon, that's for sure.

As we move into midlife, being (or becoming) alone happens even more. For many different reasons, the experience of being alone often begins to surface in midlife and seems to increase as we move into old age. Many client discussions around the struggles at this stage are frequently tied to a deep fear of ending up alone. Over the years, I've heard countless stories from clients navigating this difficult terrain of aloneness:

> ➤ The newly separated woman, terrified she will never find another partner or have the chance to have children
> ➤ The man worn down by endless dates that end with, 'It's not you, it's me'
> ➤ The single mother lying awake between her two children, wondering if she will ever get the opportunity to date again
> ➤ The 65-year-old who, after a separation, moves in with his adult daughter and her family
> ➤ The 40-year-old woman who feels despondent because she still hasn't met 'the one'

- The confused woman whose husband of over a decade has left her for someone else
- The newly divorced man who quickly leaps into another relationship with the same type of partner who isn't right for him
- The unhappily married woman too fearful to leave, worried about what solitude might bring
- The widow still reeling from the heartbreak of losing the love of her life.

It's a cacophony of aloneness that's never wanted but is, somehow, inevitable. We will likely all experience this kind of aloneness at some point.

Sometimes 'aloneness' happens quickly, sometimes it creeps up on us, sometimes we want it and sometimes we don't. People end up by themselves for many reasons and then can end up lonely for even more reasons. But it's not being alone that's the issue; it's the feeling of loneliness that hurts. And the truth is, you can still feel lonely even when you're not alone.

Chapter 4

Lonely But Not Alone

One of my clients, Mal, was a handsome, well-put-together man in his mid-forties — fit, disciplined and quietly spoken. When he wasn't working as a builder, he could usually be found at the gym or spending time with his kids. On the surface, he looked as if he had it all under control, but beneath his calm exterior he was like a duck swimming, paddling against the current. He had recently gone through a separation from his wife, the woman he had been with since he was 16. They had grown up together, built a family and shared more than two decades of life together, but the relationship had long since run its course. The tail end of the relationship had been difficult, marked by disconnection and unspoken resentment, the kind of quiet endurance that keeps people together for the sake of the kids. They spent over a year still living under the same roof, trying to hold it together until their daughters were old enough to handle time between two homes.

When Mal first came to see me, he was weighed down by plenty of the negative emotions so common when dealing with a difficult ex-partner. They were at odds over parenting arrangements, and it was exacerbated by financial disagreements. Over time, it became clear that his ex was being manipulative and unreasonable, something the courts eventually began to recognise too. Once things settled legally and he finally moved into his own place, there was a moment when he could have taken a breath—giving himself the time to rediscover who he was outside of being someone's husband or father. But instead, almost instinctively, he jumped straight into another relationship with a woman he'd met on a dating app. And strangely, she seemed just like his ex: same personality traits, same dynamics, just a different face.

It was fascinating, but also sad. Mal had spent his entire adult life attached to someone, moving from his parents' home into a relationship that had lasted more than 20 years, and then moved straight into another relationship without allowing any space in between to truly find himself. He didn't yet know what life looked like without being defined by a relationship, or who he was when he wasn't orbiting around someone else's needs or moods. He was a genuinely good, grounded man, but he had never actually met himself outside of that familiar chaos. Without that gap, that pause for self-discovery, he had unknowingly recreated the same story with a different character.

Mal isn't the first client I've seen repeat patterns or chase what feels familiar, and I doubt he'll be the last. It's something many of us do, often without realising it. We're drawn to the people, dynamics and environments that mirror what we've known, even when what we've known hasn't always been good for us. There's a comfort in the familiar. We all have our own versions of the 'familiar' that we gravitate back to—the same kind of partner, the same emotional patterns, the same situations that recreate the same feelings. Sometimes it can trace back to a parent. It's only when we pause long enough, when we give ourselves the space to be alone and truly reflect, that we can start to see the pattern for what it is, and choose differently next time.

Loneliness doesn't always stem from the absence of a partner; it can exist right smack in the middle of a relationship. The truth is that many people are in relationships and yet they feel lonely. Romantic relationships can be a source of both the most positive and the most negative experiences in our life. Many of us aspire to be in some sort of romantic relationship not long after puberty, with an almost evolutionary push to be with another. For a lot of us, we attach a whole heap of goals, expectations and dreams to this aspiration. Sometimes it works, with both partners feeling fully integrated and content in a relationship, so their relationship is everything they hoped for and more. But there is also the potential for relationships to unintentionally become a partnership of discontent and loneliness, experienced by one partner or both.

With my clients, I often find myself thinking, 'This person is such a cool human'. They're witty, thoughtful and interesting, and seem like someone who would be an awesome partner for so many people. Yet here they are, stuck in a relationship where that version of themselves doesn't shine through. It's almost like I get to see the side of them that their partner can't, or won't, see. And it makes me wonder how many people are caught in this same situation—staying in relationships that leave them distressed, disillusioned and, all too often, disconnected from not only their partner but themselves. And, because this is their daily reality, they believe it is their full reality (and the extent of their potential), with nothing different likely to happen beyond their experience of this reality. The way they are with their current partner is likely to repeat if they are with another partner. This is it.

As a mental health practitioner, I often feel that my views about relationships are somewhat skewed to the negative, or at least a little biased, in that I listen to so many unhappy stories within relationships. Therapists like me often hear the concerns, the issues and the problems that people are experiencing within their relationships—stories that clients would never tell anyone else in their life. We get to hear what goes on behind the façade of the picture-perfect relationships that are all around us, and we have the privilege of getting to understand what people are *really* experiencing and how they *really* feel about it. Over the years, I have seen far too many people that are not content at all in their relationships. It's sad to see two people staying in a relationship when they would be so much happier out of it. Yet this is what we do in society—we stay in relationships for far too long because that's what we are supposed to do.

There are many reasons why people feel lonely in a relationship. The most common concerns I have seen revolve around an emotional disconnection of sorts, whether that is due to a sudden disruption to the couple's connection or via a slow decline over the years. One of the big causes of this emotional disconnection is the unhelpful communication habits of one or both partners. Sometimes these unhelpful habits have been there all along, but they only emerge once the highs of new love settle into a familiar groove, time moves on or even challenging life events disrupt the normalcy.

Full disclaimer: I'm not a couple's therapist, but I have spent many an hour getting one half of a story from a partner—tales of why the other partner is contributing to the downfall of the relationship. Sometimes I hear about a partner who no longer listens, preferring their phone or the TV as their main source of entertainment over their partner. They are tuning in to tech and tuning out of interacting with a real person. Then there are tales of people who get aggressive or defensive when issues arise. Other times, one person might change the topic when the other person wants to talk about something important, interrupt them before they finish speaking or be too quick to offer a solution without giving them the space they need to simply validate the feelings they're trying to express (and it's not just men that are guilty of this). Some partners dismiss or minimise emotions, criticise or judge, or bring up old mistakes instead of staying in the present (like that ever works). Others might dominate the conversation, make everything about themselves, use sarcasm or passive-aggressive comments, or just avoid difficult conversations altogether. Over time, these habits can create distance, leading to one or both partners feeling disconnected from the other.

Inevitably, challenges and even tragedies happen in life that people in a relationship experience together; however, when one or both people don't want to deal with the problem, each challenging experience is left to fester, widening a disconnect or creating a distance that wasn't there before. Sometimes people are so comfortable with the disconnection in their relationship that it's too uncomfortable to confront the situation, which renders them separate but still together, leaving one or both feeling lonely.

Of course, people change across their lifespan, and most of us are certainly not like who we were 30, 20 or even 10 years ago. So, it's not unreasonable to suggest that people disconnect over time because they change—and that's okay. I'm certainly not the same person I was 30 years ago, and it makes me wonder: if I'd stayed in the same relationship all this time, how would it have evolved? Would we have grown together or apart? Would we still be a 'we' today, or might the people we've since become have made a continued relationship impossible?

It's also bloody challenging to separate. Given the logistics and the practicalities of marriage, children, businesses and whatever else we have created with our partners, it's often a big deal to separate or get divorced. It's mostly just an awful process—so much so that people will stay partnered up, despite the obvious problems. This was more common in previous generations (and is still common in some cultures) because divorce was so frowned upon. However, with the cost-of-living pressures we experience today, many people still feel they have no choice but to stay under the same roof with someone they are no longer connected to—at least for the time being.

When we're not in a relationship and feeling unhappy about it, it's easy to look at couples and think that they're in love, connected and happy. I think a lot of alone-without-a-partner people, who are feeling lonely, don't realise (or perhaps forget) that not feeling connected to a partner can feel just as lonely. Alone can mean different things to different people. As Andrea, one of my clients (who is in a relationship, mind you), says, she only dreams of having *alone time*. Seems we can't always get what we want.

We often grieve the *idea* of a relationship, rather than the reality of it. But as a single person who has a lot of insight into the lives of many partnered people, I'm telling you: it's better, for many people, to be alone rather than *lonely in a relationship*. If only they would give being alone a chance! The good news is, whether we're lonely and not in a relationship or lonely and in a relationship, there are many things we can do to not feel lonely.

So, let's start relishing that time alone.

Chapter 5
Solitude Can Save You

In my professional work, I spend much of my time designing and delivering seminars and workshops at workplace and industry events. These sessions push the message that mental wellbeing needs just as much attention as our physical health, as well as how important it is to incorporate healthy rituals into our day so we can be our best selves. One of the most popular presentations, which seems to resonate with how people are feeling these days, is on how to manage stress and prevent burnout (or, if they're already at the breaking point of burnout, how to recover from it). I talk about the contributing factors on the job and in some industries, and how some workplace systems place heavy demands on their employees. One's environment—the context in which an individual exists—contributes enormously to stress levels; unrealistic workplace expectations, excessive workload demands, unsupportive work environments, toxic cultures, unhelpful management, not feeling psychologically safe in the workplace and a lack of support can physically, mentally, emotionally and spiritually exhaust people. This exhaustion lasts not just for days, but sometimes for weeks or months. I've worked with people so burned out from their jobs that the wind of who they once were has been knocked out of them. They are physically there but psychologically elsewhere (for a bit, anyway).

Employers must take responsibility for the health and wellbeing of their most important asset—their people. However, it's crucial that we take responsibility for our own health and wellbeing too. We need to be able to manage the ebb and flow of our lives by having good self-awareness, managing our emotions (particularly our stress levels), and steering our actions and behaviours in ways that support our health and wellbeing. This may mean taking the reins of our life a little more: taking time off when we need it, saying no to things that don't work for us anymore (or that we simply don't want to do) and saying yes to the things we truly want to be doing—the things we know are the best for ourselves. It also might mean getting up earlier to stretch, making time to talk and walk in the middle of the day, going to sleep on time, eating lunch away from our desk, spacing our video calls out so we have a break in between them, or even taking the sick leave and annual leave that we're due.

Prioritising our health and wellbeing sometimes means stopping and retreating from the world and its people, just for a little while. It's a pause from the demands placed on us, where we don't talk to anyone and we're not at the beck and call of what society tells us we *should* be doing. During this temporary 'check out' of sorts from other human beings, we can relax, re-energise and rejuvenate ourselves but also reset. It's a time to listen to what our soul has been trying to tell us—what it's been trying to tell us for a while.

To show the importance of stopping (in silence), and to make the further point that it's bloody hard to do sometimes, I always do a little activity with my audiences. I instruct everyone in the audience to get comfortable in their chair, with their eyes open. The anticipation builds because they think they are about to slip into a nice meditation or even an activity of sorts (I can see the introverts looking uncomfortable, ready to run). But the only activity for the next five minutes is for them to sit in the chair quietly and *do nothing*. Simple enough, you might think—but it's almost impossible for most people (or incredibly uncomfortable, at least). In that small window of mere minutes, which seems to be an illusionary stretch of hours, they can't talk to anyone, do their work, listen to a podcast, check their emails or, God forbid, scroll on their phone. They must sit in silence.

You can see on their faces just how challenging it is. The brain, so used to a constant stream of incoming sensory information, is searching for stimulation somewhere: counting the slats in the boardroom blinds, homing in on the patterns on the never-looked-at carpet or even nervously watching me watching them. It's quite profound to witness; people realise just how difficult it is to stop, even for just five minutes. When the gruelling pause is over, I suggest to the participants that if they found the activity challenging, it's crucial that they try to do it more often.

Modern-day human beings find it incredibly difficult to just sit in silence. It's almost impossible. Think back to primary school, when you'd have to sit on a mat with your class for story time. It was pretty much impossible for a classroom full of kids to sit there and do nothing. You could see the kids around you, particularly the little boys, flicking someone in front of them. Or girls would be playing with other girls' hair. Or someone would be counting the sand grains on the rug or picking fluff off their school jumper. I can't imagine kids these days, with all their devices and whatnot, being able to sit quietly on a mat, because they certainly couldn't do that when I was at school. But it's not just the kids who have dwindling attention spans—as adults, we find it incredibly difficult too. Being alone without scrolling on a phone, turning on the TV, or putting on the radio or a podcast is a kind of deathly silence for lots of people. Too much to bear.

But so much magic happens when we stop and sit in silence without everybody else's input coming into our internal world. Many of us have not had the chance to figure out if it's a good thing for us, especially as so many of us avoid the silence of solitude. I wouldn't be the first person that's filled that gap of solitude way too quickly when I've broken up with someone—that nothingness, with no connection to anyone, just feels so strange. You can feel your mind try to pull something from your surrounding environment via your senses—something to smell, something to see, something to hear, something to taste or something to touch—just to stimulate the mind from the external world, rather than tapping into what's internal.

The Cambridge Dictionary defines solitude as 'the situation of being alone without other people'. This is something that many of us introverts crave; in fact, we can suffer when we don't have it. We still need people, of course, and need connection, but we also need a considerable amount of time to rejuvenate, recharge and recalibrate without people around. Extroverts, on the hand, get their energy from being around people. They are charged up by their connection to others, but they fall harder if they're alone too long and can't tap into a source of energy. Despite this, I would still argue that sitting in solitude would make a difference to them.

Some of us love solitude a little too much, and I include myself in that. At times, my social life seems to interrupt my solitude far too often. I almost get a little wave of disappointment when I'm invited to something because my time alone is so valuable to me: 'What … you want me to come to that?' I recently discovered that I'm not alone here. 'Otroverts' are a newly recognised personality type, introduced in recent years by psychiatrist Rami Kaminski (I devoured his book *The Gift of Not Belonging*...I've never felt so seen). Otroverts are driven by a deep desire to be alone. We don't avoid social interaction per se, and we are friendly, caring and likeable, but, unlike others, we don't crave the sense of belonging that many people need. I don't crave a sense of belonging or thrive in groups; in fact, I often find traditional social events, networking or large gatherings unappealing (and need a considerable amount of 'me' time afterwards to get my energy back). I will go to social events, but I don't have a natural calling to go and I don't have the urge to organise them. So, don't be offended if you don't get invited to a party I'm at; it's likely that I didn't organise it and I don't want to be there either. What I value far more are deep, meaningful, one-on-one connections, something big groups rarely offer. Solitude isn't something I retreat to; it's where I gravitate towards, so I can feel most like me. I'm content in my own company.

Whatever personality type we are, being alone, whether we like it or not, can still be beneficial—if we'd give it half a chance. We need to stop and see what magic happens and what our mind does when we give it space. As a writer, if I don't have that space and silence, and if I don't have that disconnection from the world, how do I know who I truly am, what I really have to say and what I want to create? I think a lot of creatives need that time out of the world to contemplate their own feelings and thoughts about life. Without this time, their creations would not actualise. In his book *Greenlights*, the Texan actor Matthew McConaughey describes how important time in solitude is for our mindset—how he takes himself away from civilisation on purpose to tap into something internal that is so important, and which gives us 'room to reveal ourselves'.

Western societies, although individualist, seem to perceive solitude as a disconnection of sorts that should be avoided. However, Eastern societies, which tend to be more collectivist in culture, see solitude as crucial to wellbeing and a strength, as it provides time for reflection and is necessary to reach a higher level of consciousness. The concept of 'yutori' in Japan means 'room', 'relaxation' or 'mental space'. It seems more pertinent than ever in a world that is fast-paced, way too busy and endlessly yells at us through technology. Yutori embodies the art of creating physical and mental space for rest, reflection and deliberate living, which does involve intentionally disconnecting socially (for a while, at least). It encourages us to slow down so we can return to balance and clarity. I can imagine the burnout statistics lowering in Western societies if we started incorporating more yutori into our way of living—giving ourselves the time and space to get clear on what we need in our life to be our best selves.

How do we know who we are if we've never even spent time with ourselves? How do we know what our soul truly wants if we've never listened to it without the influence of others? How do we know what we truly believe or even value beyond the persuasive input of the people around us? How can we know how to create contentment in our lives if we haven't learned to create it ourselves? The external world won't stop talking, and unless you tap out for a bit, you won't hear what your internal world has been whispering to you.

The most important relationship you will ever have in your life is the one that you have with yourself. And yet many of us haven't stopped to spend enough time in that relationship; we haven't had even a week of dating ourselves. Some people will only put their relationship with themselves first once a romantic relationship has ended. I see this all the time in midlifers, and I have written about it myself in a prior book, *Crisis to Contentment: The Getting of Wisdom, Mid-Life*. Many people go through their whole lives living through other people (rather than living through themselves)—they live through their family as they grow up, then they live through their peers (searching for an identity and trying on different personas). Then, by some evolutionary propellant, we seek out a mate … and so we jump into relationships. If one of these relationships fits, we stay with this person for however many years. If we have children, we look after them and hide parts of ourselves in the process. It might be the wild, fun, free person of your young adulthood that you hide away. Some of these parts of ourselves can lie dormant for years, even decades, until a separation occurs (or perhaps when the kids leave home and people become empty nesters). It is only then that we might find these parts of ourselves again—somewhere in the quietness, in the solitude, where we can hear the whispers of who we truly are, away from the noise of other people. Humans are pack animals and we often need to belong, but if we want to self-actualise and not be in survival mode all the time then we need to (and often can) step away from the pack—just for a little while.

And we need the solitude to do this.

While loneliness and social isolation are social problems that need attention—as they are linked to poor psychological and physical health problems—solitude is not a social problem. In fact, we should be encouraging it into our lives. It's something I even tell my 'not alone' people (that is, those in relationships) to do more of, urging them to engage in what researchers call 'positive solitude'. A study by Rodriguez, Schertz and Kross, published in *Nature Communications* in 2025, found that US news headlines are 10 times more likely to frame being alone negatively than positively. Society seems to put a fear of solitude in people's minds, so much so that when it happens, they jump straight out of it. But it may be the thing we need most so we can think, heal and learn. People who are constantly around people who are demanding something from them, all day every day, yearn for this time. I've had clients tell me how they put on a façade all day at work, which means they spend hours of their day being totally out of alignment with who they truly are—wearing a mask. Solitude removes the masks, the façades and the acts, giving you the time to be you…warts and all. And spending time in solitude gets you thinking.

Real solitude directs us inwards, giving us time to disconnect from the external and figure things out for ourselves. Solitude invites us to slow down, reflect and simply do what feels right for us, without performing for anyone else. It's a chance to be emotionally present for ourselves, rather than for others. When we embrace solitude in this way, the rewards are tangible: we feel rested and renewed, we gain clarity and emotional steadiness, and we discover a deeper sense of freedom and self-connection. If you sit in solitude for a while and feel the loneliness, you will start to discover such valuable information about yourself that you no longer need to feel lonely.

Just as nurturing relationships with others is vital for our wellbeing, so too is nurturing the relationship we have with ourselves.

So, let's spend some more time in that relationship.

Part II

From Heartbreak to Healing

We've got to wade through the messiness of all the emotions and find some sort of life raft for a while, until we land in a new place.

Chapter 6
The Messiness of Heartbreak

'Very MINUTE'.

On his regular visits to our childhood home, my grandfather would bellow this out to my mother from his favourite chair in our lounge room, while she prepared leftovers of meat, gravy and vegetables for him to take home. Pronounced 'my-noot' as in the smallest of portions (not 'min-ut' as in a portion of time), he'd wave his hand to warn that he only wanted the tiniest of plates to take with him and didn't want to be overfull.

'I'm full as a goog', he'd add in his Blackpudlian accent, fully aware that she was defiantly overfilling his plate. Knowing he didn't eat well on his own (likely consuming too many 'liquid nutrients', if you know what I mean), she would pile his plate high with food and wrap it carefully in aluminium foil, hoping that he'd have some sort of nourishment for the next few days. Each week, the same routine played out; he'd reluctantly take the plate from her hands, let out a sigh, roll his eyes and mumble, in an exaggerated Snagglepuss (the cartoon cat) drawl, 'Heavens to Murgatroyd' for comedic effect, which amused us grandkids. It was his way of turning his obstinance into a little performance, and my brother and I never tired of it. Each act would leave us giggling and waving as he, a 76-year-old man, sped off home on his motorbike. My grandfather—or 'Pop', as he was affectionately called—didn't want any fuss. He never stayed long and was always itching to be home for the 5 pm news.

For the 15 years I knew my grandfather, he was alone. I was three when my grandmother died, so I only have the faintest memories of her—the scent of Oil of Ulay on her skin, and her loud, chesty laugh. I hear that she adored us grandkids. I'm not sure if the pictures I have in my head are from the time I spent with her in those first few years of my life or if I've created false memories of her from poring over family photo albums since then, giving her a familiarity that may not have had time to develop in real life. In her early sixties, she passed away during a routine operation that everyone expected her to walk out of, robbing her of the time to watch her grandchildren grow up and leaving her adult children and my grandfather bereft. So, my real childhood memories of my grandparents are mostly of Pop, because we had so much more time together. And he was quite the character.

'Mr Mcgillicuddy Schicklgruber and Marrrrrrrrny Annnnnnnnnnn' he'd yell from his veranda, as my younger brother and I skipped up the pathway to his house on our visits. My brother was lucky; he was granted the funny nicknames, while I was stuck with my actual boring names, albeit in a stretched-out form. I don't remember him ever referring to or calling my brother by his actual name. Like so many of my grandfather's nicknames and sayings, they were made up just for us, much to our delight—perhaps for the sheer pleasure of how they rolled off the tongue. He used to repeat little phrases, sometimes from another language, to give us a hint of what he had learned or even experienced (but never talked about) in earlier periods of his life. I recently learned that the Allies in

World War II employed the name 'Schicklgruber' (Adolf Hitler's father's birth surname) in their propaganda to mock and undermine Hitler's authority, so perhaps his use of this name was a throwback to comradely banter with his naval mates during his years as a ship gunner in the war. Regardless of the whereabouts of his sayings (the fact that my little brother had the same nickname as Hitler was lost on us), as little kids we found his nonsensical word choices very silly indeed. It was even better when his false teeth would clumsily clunk out of his mouth as he spoke.

Our grandfather was a one-man show. He was mostly alone, and I only knew him as that, but he always seemed keen to 'exit stage left' (again, said the same way as Snagglepuss), so the assumption was that he was content that way. He seemed to have healthy ways of being alone. Much to my mother's despair, he had his motorbike, but he also spent time tinkering with his home brew, telling dirty jokes to the shopkeepers at the local supermarket, playing oom-pah beer songs on his record player, walking around the local golf course collecting lost golf balls (to then sell back to the golfers who had lost them in the first place) and picking fresh freesias for me during his walks. Other times, he had some unhealthy ways of being alone, such as retreating from us all and drinking far too much. I often wonder what he was really *feeling* back then—what was going on in his mind? I was too young at the time to wonder what was going on for someone who had lost their partner of decades. He was just alone to me. And that was that. If I was the age I am now back then, I'd have thought a little deeper about it at the time. I would have thought, 'I wonder if his heart broke when she died? I wonder if he misses her still? I wonder if the pain is getting easier to bear? I wonder if he has any regrets? I wonder if he still talks to her in his own way? I wonder if he feels her presence sometimes? I wonder if certain songs bring back memories of her?'

Whatever he felt, I do know that his journey without her wasn't easy. Thirteen years later, she came back to him—not in life, but in the quiet of his bedroom at the hospice. 'Mama's come to see me', he told us softly, while we sat with him in his final days. Soon after, he slipped away, as though following her. But he didn't leave without giving us a tearful smirk days later, leaving handwritten words on the envelope that contained his Last Will and Testament…'Gone with the Wind'.

For many people who experience loss, the journey isn't easy. And the journey from losing your partner to getting to some place where you can begin to find your footing again looks different for everyone. There is no one-size-fits-all approach to it; we've got to wade through the messiness of all our emotions and find some sort of life raft for a while, until we land in a new place.

The emotional impact of a breakup can mirror the grief we feel when we lose a loved one. The impact of a loved one's departure, whether through death or a breakup, is literally life-changing. One moment they're present in both the physical and psychological sense; the next, they're gone physically, yet still very much present in the mind and heart. While death and breakups are very different experiences, at their core they both carry the weight of loss. Someone who was once a part of your life is no longer there, leaving you to navigate the space their absence creates, as well as the thoughts and emotions associated with them. For many people, like my grandfather, navigating 'aloneness', as well as a host of other emotions associated with the heartbreak of losing someone, is all too common. It's a hodgepodge of feelings. It's all well and good to say, 'Hey, relish in solitude and be more alone, it's good for you', but it's hard to hear when you're in the depths of grief. That's why it's important that we talk about grief and heartbreak.

However you lose someone—whether they pass away or you break up, amicably or otherwise—the loss of someone who was such a huge part of your life can feel peculiar. Think back to some of the behaviours you may have displayed after your first broken heart. It's likely you were acting out of character—your mind driving you in all sorts of directions, trying to make sense of new terrain.

Heartbreak is one of the hardest things we go through as humans. It can leave us feeling completely lost and overwhelmed, doubting everything we thought we knew. And the truth is, it's messy. It can be ugly. It can be raw. One day you feel like you're coping; the next, you feel like you're falling apart. One minute you're laughing with friends; the next, you're crying alone under your blanket. One day you're confident about stepping into the 'new you'; the next, you're drowning your sorrows with one too many vodkas. One day you're swiping on Tinder; the next, you're swearing off relationships forever. That's just how it goes. It's chaotic, it's unpredictable and it's part of the process. Even years later, in a quiet moment—even if you're with a future partner—you may still have moments when your mind wanders to a love that was lost. Your reflections may be tinged with a bit of heartache and even a hint of regret. This is the humanness of relationships.

Breakup grief also pulls us deep into the complex landscape of love and loss. It's a natural reaction to the end of a romantic relationship and reflects just how much of ourselves we invest in our partners. As social beings, we build strong emotional bonds with our partners—bonds that bring us intimacy, support and companionship. We 'attach' to them. When those ties are broken, whether by choice or circumstance, we're left with a painful rupture in our emotional world. The result is often a profound sense of confusion and sorrow, which creates a wound that takes a while to heal: a wound that will likely leave a scar.

Grief over losing someone is such a deeply personal experience. We need to sit in it for a while, wade in the emotional depths of it (whatever that looks like) in our own time frame and, eventually, find our own meaning from the experience. Then, when we're ready and have dusted ourselves off, we can apply this meaning to our lives.

For those of us who are left behind, life does go on … but it's always different from what came before.

Chapter 7

Sitting with a Broken Heart

'He's such a dickhead'.

This was my client, Lucy, referring to her ex-husband, after a year of mourning the loss of him. She didn't *lose him* lose him, as he is very much alive and now living with another woman. Calling him 'a dickhead' meant that she'd finally become angry rather than forlorn, so I saw progress. Lots of it. Lucy, along with her heart, which had been torn apart, had been merely existing since their marriage had ended — going through an assortment of emotions one would expect after a shock separation.

I had been seeing Lucy for about six months, coaching her through some workplace issues. We were firmly focused on her unreasonable workloads, recent organisational upheaval and some dodgy management decisions, homing in on building her confidence and communication strategies so she could navigate it all. Personal issues often crop up in professional coaching sessions, even though we are talking primarily about workplace issues, but she reported that everything at home was fine, and there were no complaints about her husband. She presented as a happily married woman. There was no clue as to what would happen next.

When her husband initiated the sheepish conversation in which he announced he was leaving (dancing around the fact that he had met someone else), Lucy was completely blindsided. His revelations of long-standing unhappiness and his need for time and space to 'find himself' left her confused. He was even using language that he'd never used before—'"Find himself"? WTF!' Lucy was baffled. They were a couple, they were each other's 'person', they had a family, and here he was talking about leaving to go and 'find himself'. He spoke of renting a unit nearby to think, again insisting that he had not met anyone else—though no matter what she asked, and no matter how hard she tried to understand, his words offered little clarity. She was left to flounder in their family home.

The initial shock of it all gradually gave way to deeper confusion. Lucy tried to piece together the fragments of his explanations over the months, to force them into some kind of coherent narrative, but nothing quite fit. It was all so unlike him. She swung between disbelief and denial, clinging to the hope that perhaps this was all temporary, a midlife crisis of sorts. She had hope, and then she didn't. She wanted him back, and then she didn't. She thought he might have depression, and then she didn't. He cruelly gave her only breadcrumbs of information about his reasons for leaving, never the full truth, leaving her oscillating between hope and despair. Her emotions were all over the place.

When we don't get the truth (or any information, for that matter), people start to fill in the gaps, which can be unhelpful at times. We can only use what we know—and what we mostly know about is ourselves, which makes us wonder what we could have done differently. Eventually, after a few months, Lucy sank into sadness, a deep, lingering sorrow she attributed to her own perceived failings—as a woman, as a wife, as someone who had somehow perhaps not been enough. Anger did not surface for some time; it was buried beneath layers of hurt and grief, waiting silently for the right moment to emerge.

And when it did, I was pleased. Progress! After many discussions and reflection sessions with me, Lucy took off the rose-coloured glasses and realised that perhaps he wasn't the kind-hearted husband she'd thought he was. Yes, there were plenty of happy memories, but there were many moments in their relationship when he'd treated her pretty damn poorly, and she'd been rationalising her way through it for far too long. Wading through the pot of emotions in the broken-hearted phase, then acknowledging that her husband had indeed been 'a dickhead' (even during the marriage), helped to cushion the blow somewhat by the time the revelation about the new girlfriend came along. But to get to that stage, she needed to take the time to sit with that pot of emotions. You can't fast-track your way through a broken heart. Every single emotion that comes up, even if it's different every single day, is valid.

If you've got at least a handful of romance books on your bedside table, or stacked neatly on your bookshelf, you're certainly not alone. Romance novels are the top-selling genre of fiction books globally and, like many avid readers, I'm here for them. There's nothing like lying in bed at night with a cat on your lap, a cup of tea by your side and a romance novel in your hand. What more could anyone want? Romance novels are a billion-dollar industry, with their universal plots of love (and lust) resonating with so many of us. These are stories that we live for, hope for and want more of. Some of us might get a taste of the tales of lust and love depicted in their pages but, for the most part, these books are the stuff of dreams. In some ways, these novels prepare us a little in case such dreams come to fruition.

Call me a mental health professional who has heard plenty of real-life stories (because I am), but who prepares us for when the heart is broken? What happens when the love dies and the lust fades? What happens when instead of staring into your soul, she's staring into her phone? What do you do when instead of slamming you into a wall in a moment of passion, he's sleeping on the couch or in the spare room? What do you do when instead of seductively biting her lip when you walk into a room, she's irritably clenching her teeth? None of us are buying books about these realities of being in a relationship, which happen more often than we think. This is not part of the fantasy at all, even though it often becomes the reality.

'Till death do us part' is one of the most well-known wedding vows. It implies that when we enter a marriage, we expect it to last a lifetime, with the marriage ending only when one half of the couple passes away. In the case of more than 50 per cent of marriages, 'Till death do us part' isn't exactly true. As romantic as those words sounds when they come out of our mouths at the altar, most people part ways long before anyone passes away.

A range of feelings hit us when we are heartbroken…feelings of disillusion, letdown, frustration, desperation, devastation, sadness, disappointment, panic, fear and even anger. Depending on the nature of the breakup (whether it was expected or unexpected; who initiated the breakup), you may also feel jealousy, confusion and regret. Some of us default to thinking it's all the other person's fault or it's all our fault. We might not feel good enough; we may even feel worthless, which rocks our self-esteem and tramples all over our self-worth. Our hopes and dreams have been dashed in the blink of an eye, and we didn't even have a say in it. We might start asking ourselves, 'Why has this happened?' If we don't have all the answers, sometimes the only definite we have is ourselves—which is why it's so easy to think it is because of us. Don't even get me started on how triggering this can be if a similar situation has happened in the past (I talk more about such emotional baggage in Chapter 9).

Emotions can be felt in the body. I've had clients tell me they feel numb, exhausted or as if they are in shock. The heaviness in the chest is real; the heart is literally aching. There is even a condition called broken heart syndrome. In an article published in 2008 in the *American Heart Journal*, Prasad *et al* speak of 'takotsubo cardiomyopathy', which is a weakening of the left ventricle, the heart's main pumping chamber. The condition is usually a result of severe emotional or physical stress—such as a sudden illness, a serious accident or the loss of a loved one—causing classic heart attack symptoms, including pain in the chest, heaviness and severe pressure. The precise cause of broken heart syndrome isn't known, but experts think that surging stress hormones (for example, adrenaline) essentially 'stun' the heart, triggering changes in heart muscle cells or coronary blood vessels that prevent the left ventricle from contracting effectively.

Separation can be an emotionally turbulent period, and its effects can linger for months or even years, especially when financial matters or arrangements for children complicate matters. Strong emotions arise at each email from the lawyer, phone call from the ex and text message from your child when they are at your ex's house. It is understandable for emotions to be to-ing and fro-ing for quite some time.

There's much to be said for sitting in emotional pain: eating ice-cream in our pyjamas on the couch while watching old romance movies and doing nothing. Crying on the phone to our friends. Playing Whitney Houston songs on repeat. Packing your ex's stuff in cardboard boxes and throwing them out the window. All of which are healthier than putting on a façade and getting on with it. The longer we avoid the feeling, the more we delay our healing. We have to walk through it all and feel it. Yes, we might want to numb it, ignore it, deny it or even sweep it under the rug. It may work for a while, but none of this will help in the long term. Sitting in the depths of despair, however uncomfortable it makes you feel, allows you the time to process what's happened. It's painful in the short term to feel this way but you will be better for it in the long run.

Being open and honest about whatever your heartbreak looks like and feels like will help you, even if it feels chaotic. You won't always feel like talking about it, and I get that (I'm not a big talker about things—I know I'm not supposed to say this as a mental health professional, but it's true). But talking and debriefing about your experience helps. Talking helps you think and make sense of things. It helps you process the range of emotions that you feel. Family and friends can be helpful at times, but it also helps to talk to mental health professionals because they are trained to guide us through life's inevitable ups and downs, including relationship challenges. They can assist people with a suite of strategies for managing emotions and unhelpful thinking loops.

Once we have waded through the emotions of our broken heart, and have had time to reflect, we often come to some realisations—namely, that the person we have lost might not have been right for us after all.

Sometimes, we realise that being with that person was just a habit, or a pattern. We have been repeating behaviours that we've been acting on since childhood, unconsciously chasing something that we may have been looking for from a parent (I know ... squirm). Maybe we have been looking for approval or acceptance from others, as that is what we've always done. Often, we lack the knowledge gained from prior experience to know what to do when people treat us badly. We may be relying on a blueprint laid in our childhood. As a therapist, I often wonder what had happened in the past to a client in order for them to think that certain behaviours are okay; sometimes I ask them, 'What happened to you?'

Navigating a broken heart can be one of the most difficult things we'll ever do. On an emotional level, it can be one of the most painful processes in our lives. Coping in a healthy way means identifying these painful feelings, allowing ourselves to experience these feelings and getting the right support. Once people have healed, many people come to the profound realisation that they have let themselves down—but now it's their time. And this is an important part of the journey.

Reflection

How are you supporting your broken heart?

Chapter 8
Healing After Goodbye

'I'll come back in six weeks for that one', I told my friends, pointing to the tiny kitten wriggling among his tiger-striped and grey siblings as they nursed from their sleeping mother.

'The black-and-white one',

And I did. Six weeks later, I returned to collect that little black-and-white kitten, and Mowgli became my sidekick for the next 20 years. He was with me through a couple of relationships, six different houses, eight other pet friends and two children. A little piece of black-and-white living furniture that moved through life right alongside me. Mowgli was never part of the plan. Choosing him felt less like deciding whether a pet was a good idea and more like recognising something I already knew deep down. Technically, if I wrote a list of pros and cons to make the decision about acquiring a cat at that moment, the cons list would have been sensibly longer. And yet, he was the best decision. A little like going away for a weekend and coming home with the keys to a house in the middle of the forest: illogical, unexpected, a little expensive but somehow exactly the right thing to do.

At the time of choosing Mowgli, I was in my early twenties, renting a house that didn't allow pets and in a relationship with a man who claimed to be allergic to cats. His allergies seemed to flare only when he saw one—which always made me suspect it was more drama than a diagnosis. As an animal lover, I'll admit my empathy has always been thin when someone recoils from cats. I mean, it's a cat. What is a cat going to do to them? I just don't get the aversion to cats (unless, of course, someone actually is allergic and it's not some sort of 'nocebo' reaction). Anyway, the relationship I was in at that point wasn't working anymore. I felt like I'd been treading water for too long; I wasn't happy, and I'd said so more than once, but I didn't yet have the gumption to end things completely. That was my first long-term relationship, and I was still building up my psychological muscles of assertion.

Then, one weekend, visiting friends whose cat had just given birth to these ridiculously cute kittens, I saw them all nestled together, their tiny bodies wriggling for space. And just like that, I knew. I wanted that kitten. I wanted the black-and-white one. And if that was going to be the impetus to let the boyfriend go, so be it. The lightbulb went on. It was the right time. I gave myself those six weeks, enough time to end the relationship and make space for Mowgli to move in. And that's exactly what happened. The boyfriend moved out, the kitten moved in, and Mowgli stayed by my side for the next two decades. The longest relationship I've had outside of my relationship with my parents.

Looking back, I sometimes shake my head at what I put up with in my younger years—the misaligned relationships, the value compromises that never sat right and the times when I was treated badly. For example, these days, with a house full of pets (not quite a menagerie, but close), I can't imagine being with someone who doesn't love animals. In fact, if someone walked into my home right now and ignored my dog's over-the-top greeting, brushed off a cat rubbing against their leg or didn't say 'hello' to my bird in a high-pitched voice, I'd have no hesitation in showing them the door.

That moment of clarity — that gut knowing — is rare, and I believe it is likely to become even rarer in the noisiness of modern life. And it can take time to realise what we value most. Values are the guiding principles that shape how we live, the choices we make and the way we respond to the world. And often, we aren't even aware of them. Sometimes we realise we've been living according to other people's values: the ones we've inherited from our parents, our friends, our culture or even long-standing societal expectations. We grow up absorbing all these values like a sponge, often not questioning any of them. Then, without noticing it, we step straight into our first relationships, absorbing the values of our partners. Over time, it can feel normal, even right, until a moment of clarity shows us otherwise. Sometimes an animal, a conversation, a music lyric, an unasked-for experience or a gut feeling has a way of holding up a mirror to what we truly want (and don't want). It cuts through the noise of logic, circumstance or fear, and nudges us towards choices that our rational mind might resist but our heart already knows are right. These are the turning points that realign us — the kitten that makes you leave a relationship, the impulse move that changes your path, the small decision that quietly shapes decades of your life. It's almost a cosmic redirection, because you were taking too long to figure it out for yourself. Often, these turning points don't look like much at the time. But, in hindsight, you see them for what they really were: the moments that set you back on course to the life you were meant to be living.

Sometimes the reasons for breaking up with someone, and instigating your own alone time, are as clear as day. It is obvious to you that it's not meant to be, and you may have psychologically checked out in some ways before you physically did. In this case, you often have had a chance to silently reconcile everything in your mind, including the impending changes, before your partner realises. Which may be better for you but, at the same time, it can create some emotional angst that you might not be prepared for. Even when it feels like the right thing to do, it can still be painful to be the one that breaks the status quo and calls quits on a relationship; just because you are in control, it doesn't mean the end is any less sad or disruptive. Putting yourself first can feel terribly uncomfortable (particularly when you're not in the habit of doing it), but knowing that your partner is going to feel emotional pain because of your decision can feel even worse, bringing on painful feelings of guilt that may sit with you for a long time (or at least until you know they are doing better). Because you are initiating the change (based on what you think, feel and predict), moving from one way of being to another, you also can't be 100 per cent sure it's for the best, so a level of ambivalence may creep up, leaving you wondering, 'Did I do the right thing?'

Being alone can give you that clarity. It's a chance to ask yourself, 'What matters to me? What doesn't matter to me? Which choices have truly been mine? Which have been reflections of someone else's world?' In those quiet moments, like the day I saw Mowgli wriggling with his litter buddies, you can recognise what resonates deep down (and even what's been missing for so long) and start making decisions that align with your own heart, even if they feel unexpected at first.

Reflection

It's hard to instigate a goodbye; are you making room for all your emotions?

Chapter 9

Claiming Your Emotional Baggage

A few years ago, my friend Sarah recommended a psychic who had provided her with spookily accurate readings over the years. She regularly visited this trusted lady for guidance about her future, particularly when she was in the depths of despair or needed a shove (in any direction) off the fence of ambivalence in major life decisions. Enjoying her stories over lunch dates (ooooh she was going to meet the perfect man in the future, she was going to travel overseas next year and there is an older woman, starting with G, who has been talking about her behind her back), I started wondering what this psychic would say to me. So, I promptly booked a session with her.

A month later, I arrived early, with anticipatory eagerness, and entered the tiniest of waiting rooms, where I sat staring at a crusty floral arrangement in a vase on top of a cream doily on a coffee table. I had a list of pertinent questions with me, a few photographs in my pocket (as requested by her) and a notebook for scribbling her observations about my future. I had practised my poker face in the car on the way. After a good 40 minutes or so, the velvet-draped psychic finally walked out and ushered me into a slightly bigger room. We sat opposite each other, and she asked for the payment first so we could concentrate for the rest of the session without worrying about the fiddly financial exchange. Once that was done, we sat for a further two minutes in silence. Her eyes were closed, and she was tuning in to whatever she was tuning in to. She then abruptly opened her eyes, told me that I had too many blocks and she couldn't read me, and then *gave me my money back*.

That was the last time I went to a psychic.

I'm grateful, though, that she didn't just keep me there for the hour and make my destiny up. That would have been worse. But I did feel a little offended when I drove away. I began reflecting on these apparent blocks I had. Was this true? Did I have blocks? I was a little bit defensive about what she said, but it did get me thinking. Am I blocking people? Is the reason that I'm alone because I'm blocking people? Could I even be blocking the right person for me? Blocks occur unconsciously for a reason, and it's usually because the brain has thought it best to take over and protect us because of a previous experience that it has deemed psychologically or physically harmful. If an experience in the present moment might end up in a similar way, the brain will make up its mind to protect you before you realise it is happening.

One could say that because I've had my heart broken, my brain is still rather overprotective of me; maybe my unconscious mind is opting for the perceived safer route of staying single. My brain is so protective of me that it has had the ability to turn my whole body around and walk me in the other direction from the mere sight of an ex, almost like a trained Navy SEAL, whose unconscious brain moves them out of danger before they consciously become aware of the danger. When you have had a particularly difficult previous relationship, it's understandable that your brain doesn't want to repeat the situation. Difficult past relationships can be hard, the loss of a loved one can be hard and, damn, broken hearts can be hard. There I was, thinking I was all fine and dandy about being single and alone, but perhaps I wasn't. It's worth thinking about, I guess. Stupid psychic.

A by-product of living life is to feel emotions. We feel emotions attached to our experiences. Some of these emotions dissipate quickly—sometimes so quickly that we don't even notice them. But other emotions are set off because of something challenging we once went through, and the brain has decided it is important enough to hold on to. It could be anything that caused your emotions to heighten: rotten treatment, horrible words, raised voices, mean phrases, lies, put-downs, passive-aggressive comments. The mind has categorised it as something that has hurt you in some way in the past and therefore may be a threat to your survival now and possibly in the future. As a result, you carry this with you going forward in life. Your emotional baggage comes along for the ride—it's the 'stored weight' of your past.

In some ways, we cling to this emotional baggage because it protects us, whether we are aware of it or not. This isn't necessarily a bad thing; as we'll explore in Chapter 10, it shapes our wisdom. But it can also become unbearably heavy, weighing us down far more than we need it to. Imagine dragging a bag behind you. If it contains something familiar, like your favourite sparkly shoes, you feel its weight and, somehow, you can manage it. You own it. But what if the bag is overstuffed with things you don't recognise, such as old grudges, unspoken regrets, fierce resentment, dishonesty or other fears you can't even name? It presses on your shoulders, pulls at you when you take small steps or even grinds you to a halt when you when you are trying to move forward. And yet, because you have no idea what's in that bag, you don't know why you feel so exhausted, why your path feels wrong, or why it seems impossible to move forward.

Going through a challenging relationship in the past (or even experiencing a great relationship with a challenging ending) can leave us carrying a whole heap of emotional baggage into the future. Maybe we consciously believe we are doing well, but we still have some unconscious residue that may affect us. For me, I need to check my emotional baggage quite often and find ways to unpack it so it doesn't feel so heavy. No wonder I get a sore back at times.

At some level of consciousness, the brain will remember everything that has psychologically or physically harmed us in the past in order to protect us — even if that means tucking the memory of these harms away, outside of our awareness. If we go about our business and we find ourselves in a scenario that 'feels' like something that has happened in the past, our brain will be triggered. A feeling will come over us that puts us in a fight, flight or even freeze state — when we behave in ways that are driven by our irrational or emotional brain, rather than our rational and thinking brain. This can affect our behaviour in and around relationships, potentially causing us to run away from them (as one example). The emotional contents of your suitcase inform how you travel along your own path: how you approach your job, how you problem-solve, how you make friends and keep them, how you speak to strangers. They influence how you view people who are different to you, drive how and why you make certain decisions, and impact how you show up in a relationship.

Claiming, appreciating and unpacking our baggage is a process that begins with awareness — with the idea that people don't do things *to us*; they do things, period, and the contents of our baggage may trigger a reaction or a response. Unpacking doesn't happen overnight, and it requires patience, courage and grace. Whether you do this with a therapist or on your own, know that you may discover a lot of emotions, and that's okay. You might become tired of bringing up these emotions, but it is helpful; you will exhaust yourself if you're constantly weighed down.

It's quite cathartic to reflect on any situations, words or behaviours that cause strong emotional reactions for you. Be curious about the emotions and see if they are tied to fear, anger, guilt, rejection or even abandonment. Once you're aware of the strong emotional reactions that you might experience now and again, it's important to dig around a little and try to understand the root cause. For me, I'm aware that if anyone tries to lock me in to a commitment, I immediately feel trapped and uncomfortable. I have a fear of becoming locked into things (such as relationships, contracts and so on). It's an irrational fear of becoming controlled, which can prevent me from taking advantage of opportunities in the present moment. It's probably why I err on the side of being a 'commitment-phobe' and I'm a little hyper-independent at times, which can be great in some ways, but I need to keep a check on it when it's to my own detriment.

You may be aware of something else that triggers a strong emotional response in you. For people who have been cheated on in the past, a partner not replying immediately may trigger anxiety. A person who has been lied to in the past may react to even the slightest hint that someone is not telling the truth, which could cause them to irrationally jump to the wrong conclusion. Someone who's been criticised constantly in a relationship might take minor feedback as personal failure. Someone who's been gaslighted in the past might react to small misunderstandings as if their reality is being questioned again. Someone who's been ignored could be triggered by even the smallest signs of inattention and feel emotional rejection.

Once you are aware of all your baggage, you can remind yourself that this is in the past, and your brain is replaying it. Then you can ask yourself, 'Is this about what's happening now, or is it just about the past?' Once you question yourself a little more and try to get into a place of self-enquiry, you can learn to calm those intense emotions when you do get triggered. Then, from a healthier emotional space, you can work on reframing those past experiences to reduce their power over you. It's empowering when you realise you can do something positive about the negative experiences and emotions you've been carrying for so long.

Everyone carries emotional baggage, but life feels lighter when you open the heaviest suitcases, sort through what's inside, leave behind what weighs you down and only take forward what truly serves you.

Chapter 10
Tapping into Your Wisdom

Male koalas have developed an interesting approach to romantic rejection by lady koalas—they just give up and go to sleep. Unlike humans, who tend to pursue, chase, seek, woo and get rather offended when it all remains unreciprocated, these cuddly marsupials don't waste any further energy chasing uninterested mates. If a female isn't receptive to their attempts to impress by busting a move, they won't persist. Instead, they give up, retreat, conserve their energy and wait for a better opportunity. Call them quitters, but according to researchers, koalas have evolved to behave in this way. Mating calls for significant effort; in a koala's world, where energy is limited by a eucalyptus-only diet, efficiency matters. Rather than fight a losing battle, male koalas opt for the biological equivalent of 'she's just not that into me' and simply go back to napping.

Us humans can certainly take a (eucalyptus) leaf out of the koala's book.

'Be more koala' is advice I would have liked many of my clients over the years to have taken when they were feeling out of sorts, particularly when they would jump straight into the dating world again after a relationship breakdown and have a terrible time as a result. It is the kind of advice I think many of us need to be onboarding. Yes, you will be rejected now and again, but that's the way life goes sometimes, so don't let it bother you when it happens; instead, spend time doing something you love to do. Another opportunity will come along eventually.

Unfortunately, one of the better (or worse, depending on how you look at it) things about being a higher order animal is that we have a rather large thinking part of our brain, so the thinking part can take over and put us in a large amount of distress. We're physically there but not mentally or emotionally in the present moment because we're worrying about the future and ruminating about the past. We might be grieving the idea of someone and the life that we had imagined we would share with them. We can't simply let it go, and it's very difficult to imagine (never mind step into) the future if we're still holding on to the past. This is why we need the space and time to tap into the learnings from our past relationships; however, taking the time to reflect and learn from our experiences does not happen often enough. We can be hurt by others, or even hurt others ourselves, without stopping to really reflect on whether we have made a mistake or not. We all make mistakes in life, but not all of them are big enough to jolt us awake so we make sure we never make the same mistake again. This is particularly true about mistakes that involve people. Sitting in the space between making a mistake and learning from the outcome is something that many of us skip over.

Most of our wisdom comes from immersing ourselves in life's richness, engaging with the messiness and daring to extract the gold from our experiences. Wisdom isn't handed to us; it's gathered over a lifetime, bit by bit, as we navigate what's hard, what's joyful and what's painfully unclear. We grow as people by living, learning and reflecting. For many of us, such wisdom is hard-earned from the adversities that shook us. Much of our learnings come from the relationships of our past. We remember those moments of crisis we thought we'd never get through, those nights of turmoil where our emotions clouded our capacity to think properly. Yet, once the dust had settled, we realised we could begin to think again, to process, to rebuild. Each time we learn from our experiences, we walk away with a kind of golden formula: a way of coping, learning and improving that shapes how we handle the next storm, relationship-based or otherwise. Wisdom gives us a guide we can draw on, one that helps us see more clearly, love more deeply and live more intentionally.

Like many of the adversities we may encounter in our lives, breakups are rarely straightforward. Sometimes the reasons are clear, and other times we're left drowning in a sea of confusion, struggling to come up for air and make sense of what happened. But even confusing experiences can hold lessons. It helps to consider: 'Why did that happen? Why did I do that? Why did I put up with that for so long? Why did I go back to him? Did I stay out of fear of being alone? What did I truly want versus what I settled for?'

Eventually, what once felt like pure heartbreak can, in hindsight, reveal truths we missed when we were deep inside the relationship. When we internalise what we've learned, the pain isn't just loss. It becomes so much more than that. It becomes growth.

Have you noticed how it's always the other person (not the one who's telling you their story) that's the difficult party when it comes to a breakup? It's always the story of what the other person did: their flaws, their choices, the part they played in the breakdown of the relationship. Sometimes other people do treat us badly, leave abruptly or break our trust. But that isn't always the full story. Often, as painful as it is to realise, we may have contributed in some way. Growth requires us to turn the mirror back on ourselves, asking difficult but important questions, such as: 'What role did I play? What drama did I feed into? What signals did I ignore?' This kind of reflection doesn't excuse the other person's actions, but it frees us to learn from our own. It gives us the opportunity to notice where we can grow, so we don't keep repeating the same patterns in new relationships. One of my clients, Peter, reflected to me one day, after spending so long blaming his wife for leaving him: 'I realised I just kept taking, taking from her, taking until she had nothing left to give'. This was an important realisation for him to have while he was alone, as it was a lesson he could learn from before he entered another relationship in the future.

When a relationship is behind you, the only person you can change is yourself. That might feel confronting, but it's also empowering. It's something to get excited about. Through something heartbreaking, you find the freedom to explore what your strengths are, where there's room to grow and what you truly want out of life. I've worked with clients who, after a fair bit of healing, have realised what they really need in a future relationship, often because they were not getting it in their previous relationship. I've worked with men who want their future partners to trust them more and I've worked with women who want to be listened to, validated and really heard. I've worked with men who want their future partner to be more independent and confident. I've worked with women who want their future partner to stay calm, reasonable and rational in conflict. And most of all, people want honesty, reliability and trustworthiness in a relationship. People want respect; they want love, support and care.

As the saying goes, hindsight is a wonderful thing, and it is a powerful gift if we choose to use it. By unpacking what happened, owning your part and deciding what you want to do differently next, you give yourself the best chance of creating healthier, more fulfilling relationships going forward: with others and, of course, with yourself.

Part III

Being Only You

Alone time with intention will give you so many unexpected gifts. It might even leave you wanting more.

Chapter 11
Relish in Your Presence

'Already? No way. I hadn't finished my book'. These are the words that elite sportswoman Beatriz Flamini uttered after spending 500 days (voluntarily, mind you) alone in a dark cave 70 metres below the Earth's surface. Once the designated time to resurface had arrived, she came across as rather unfazed about the end of her alone time. After descending into the cave in southern Spain on 20 November 2021 with the intention of understanding how the human mind and body could deal with extreme solitude in hard circumstances, Flamini seemed to have coped with aloneness quite well indeed.

For those following her journey, it seemed positively unfathomable that a human being, particularly one who is used to being a part of society, would be able to survive such solitude. Away from people, unaware of what was going on in the world (even with her own family and friends) and living alone in the dark with just the basics for living…most of us wouldn't dream of volunteering for such an experiment. We just know we wouldn't be able to do it. But she did, and she seemed to have fared well during her 500-day solo expedition of sorts. Flamini's trick to keeping well seemed to involve focusing on the present moment, living in the here and now, and actively doing things that she enjoyed. Apart from the usual daily inconveniences of living in a dark cave (such as insects, a lack of delicious food and no toilet—any of which would make many of us recoil in horror), she didn't list being alone as one of the problems. She seemed quite content to pass the time reading, writing, drawing and knitting. When questioned about how she stayed sane during her time in the cave, she told journalists that she had extensive experience and was mentally prepared, saying, 'I got on very well with myself'.

Apart from being such a courageous endeavour for any human to embark on and endure, there is something quite romantic about Flamini's experience: to be able to sit in your own company, in the presence of your own thoughts, and to be driven by how you feel in the moment without the outside world butting its nose in and influencing what you do with your time. It would be such a break from the usual grind and expectations of others to have all that stripped away. I draw the line at the creepy-crawlies, never-ending darkness and absence of a proper toilet, but it does seem quite nice to have all that time to oneself.

Over the years, I've many watched movies where aloneness has been the central theme. While watching Tom Hanks wade through crystal-clear tropical waters or traipse through an uncharted island wilderness in *Cast Away*, I thought, 'Wow, that looks rather pleasant' rather than feeling dissuaded by the solitude of his predicament. How peaceful it would be to not have anyone around you. How serene it would be to not know what's going on in the news. How relaxing it would be to not have advertisers constantly telling you to buy their stuff…and how luxurious it would be to have a clear schedule where you can do whatever you want. I'm sure many modern adults my age would agree — in principle, at least. Because yes, I'm romanticising the idea a little, as we know Tom Hanks's character had to catch his own fish, didn't have any good footwear and was deeply upset about Wilson leaving. His situation wasn't so peaceful and serene, and his life was in danger at times. But a little more time for ourselves in the present moment, filled only with things that we truly want to do, could do us all some good. As in the many movies that take us on a 'hero's journey' through discomfort and solitude, being left to your own devices to figure out what you want from the day can be beneficial and may help you come out the other side of the day a better version of yourself than you were before — even if you're a bit dishevelled from the process.

About 15 years ago, after a long time being employed by people in various organisations and institutions and then a few years working for myself, I started to think a little differently about what I wanted out of my career, and life in general. Married with two very young children at the time, and having also recently finished a professional doctorate, I was keen to learn more about how I could find the magical balance between having a career *and* being a full-time mum (I'm not sure if anyone's found the perfect recipe for that yet, but if you have, please let me know). At the time, I was on a mission to actualise this impossible feat, finding ways to hang out with the kids during the day and work in the moments when the kids were sleeping — day or night. A bit of consulting here, a bit of lecturing there, a bit of tutor marking here, a few client consultations there: I was doing bits and bobs of short contracts, casual jobs, freelancing and university sessional work all under the umbrella of my work as a mental health professional.

I was keen to learn more about how I could have a career and be a stay-at-home mum — not only then, but throughout the next 20-plus years as my children grew up. I wanted my business to work alongside my kids as they started kindergarten and entered full-time school, and then throughout high school, with all the extracurricular activities, sport trainings, playdates and first-time jobs that would likely be wrapped around it all. I was wondering how someone could create a business doing something they love, something they know the world needs and they are good at, as well as choose exactly the hours they want to work each week—all while knowing it could change at any moment. A seemingly impossible task (and this was all before working from home was a thing!).

Like many business owners, I branched away from being an employee. I started my own business because I craved autonomy. I wanted to be in control, have the freedom to do things my way and build a more flexible lifestyle (I wasn't asking for much!). But what often happens (and it happened to me a few times) is that somewhere along the way, the business begins to take control. For me, instead of creating freedom, it felt like I was chained to my business, constantly at its beck and call. I was exhausted and stretched way too thin. My aim of 'having it all' was proving to be quite ridiculous and burning me out in the process.

Before I reached total burnout, I stopped and grabbed the reins. Thinking about everything I had learned from psychology and business along the way, I sat down, alone, to think about and reflect on everything I had absorbed over the years. I then consciously started creating my psychology business in a way that truly aligned with the life I personally and professionally wanted, not the life that was expected of me. I wrote down exactly how I wanted to spend each day—from the moment I woke up to the moment I went to bed. I detailed everything I wanted to be doing, both in my personal life and in my career: what the task was (work or otherwise), when it would happen, who I would be doing it with, how long it would take and where it would take place. Yes, it involved thinking about the work that I like to do the most, but it also involved thinking about what I love to do the most in my personal life, such as spending time with the kids, weekday lunches with friends and long, lingering walks with my dog. I would visualise this life, closing my eyes and immersing myself, with all five senses, in the reality of what this life would look like: my perfect day, with me in it. I've continued this practice ever since, for more than 10 years—updating the vision regularly, almost like a living, breathing, sensory vision board in my mind. It's a mind movie I add to, remove from and revise continually, and it's been a virtual framework I've used to steer my business, and my life, since then. Reflecting on this exercise has shown me how well I have wrapped my business around my kids as they have grown, and how this exercise has paid off when it has steered me back on track when life inevitably threw me off course (and boy, did it ever—taking me the long, wiggly way many times). I have adapted my approach to life and work slowly, in real time, every time small or large changes have happened in my life.

Recently, however, I've felt a quiet, rebellious streak stirring within me, an almost silent resistance to the way I've been working: a spiritual burnout of sorts, where I have the energy to do only the things I truly want to do, and no energy to do the things that I don't, which is leading me to feel quite dissatisfied in certain areas of my life that I was quite content in before. This is a feeling that life coach Martha Beck, author of *Finding Your Way in a Wild New World*, urges her readers to tap into so they can be more in alignment with who they truly are, and do more of what they want to do in life, rather than being out of alignment and spending their lives doing things that they don't want to do. She describes the difference between the two extremes as 'shackles on' (when you are doing something your soul doesn't really want to do) and 'shackles off' (when you are doing something your soul is in alignment with).

Being middle-aged and having had more time alone, I get to really think about who I am, what I want, what I like and what I don't. It's as if you can hear your thoughts more clearly. I have more of an awareness of what I want now. It's like an inner knowing, where I can move away from the things that don't work for me anymore and move towards what I want (the career I want, the friendships I want to nurture, and so on). So, my inner rebellion is an intense feeling that says if it's not a 'hell yeah', it's a 'nah'. This is not a totally unfamiliar feeling but, in the past, I would have overridden it or even ignored it and just realigned myself to whatever the world wanted, needed or expected of me.

I began to wonder what all this unfamiliar restlessness was about. I've hypothesised that perhaps it's because my children are older now and so they're no longer as dependent on me. Now they've finished high school and are out in the world, doing their own thing more than ever before, the 'wrapping around my children' philosophy doesn't need to apply so much. After nearly two decades of parenting, time for myself is starting to slowly reappear. At some level, I had noticed that I had less commitments in the afternoons and evenings (no more school pick-ups; no more sitting at sport training sessions or waiting in car parks as casual jobs finished). What I hadn't noticed is that I don't need to spend my time trying to maintain that delicate balance anymore (however wobbly it sometimes seemed). After 19 years of child-rearing, this extra time is now mine, so I can do more of what I want to do. My subconscious mind has been telling me that I could perhaps use that time for something else that is more in alignment with who I am, or even who I am yet to become. It's been poking me on the shoulder, saying, 'Hey girl, slow down a bit, take some time for yourself. It's a time for recalibration and a new direction'.

This isn't the kind of rebellion that shouts from the rooftops; it's softer and quieter than that. In fact, many people may not notice it at all. It was a simple realisation: I just want to do more of what I want to do. Although I'm excited to have had this realisation, it's another thing altogether to sit in the sombre realisation that Rome wasn't built in a day. I'm still in the overlap of what I was doing before. Future me is following my bliss and absolutely having a blasting time of it: 'Hey, future me—look at you!' But for now, that time in between—the gap, the interspace, the silence, the presence—is where I need to be to recalibrate, reset and restart. It's where I will find the clues to my future self. And this is where I will be sitting for a while.

In a world that feels fast-paced, uncertain, volatile and ambiguous, slowing down and grounding ourselves in the present moment feels less like a luxury and more like a necessity. It gives us back the reins in a time when so much feels out of our control. In our own company, we can have quiet moments when no one is demanding anything from us, no one needs us to fix anything or carry their burdens, and no one is pulling our attention in directions we might not want to go. During time alone, we get to choose what we allow in to reach our senses—what we see, hear, touch, taste and smell. We can control the flow, the inputs and the pace, eliciting a feeling of freedom (in German, the word for this is *sturmfrei*—when you are 'storm-free', with the house to yourself). And in that space, time itself seems to slow down. The noise of the world—its arguments, its constant comparisons on social media, its endless cycle of outrage—falls away, and in its place is a quiet that feels like alignment. We are alone, but both psychologically and physically we're in the same place.

In the present moment, there is a silence. If you let it linger for a while, it allows you to start remembering who you are, without expectation and without performing for anyone else. The more you immerse yourself in this silence, the more you might crave it. I know I do. As they say, silence is golden. Being alone in the silence is a golden opportunity to do the things that you totally want to do, without the world interfering. At first, that freedom can feel uncomfortable, almost odd, and the temptation is to fill it with a person—especially for those who aren't used to being alone. But time and again I've seen clients move past that initial unease and discover just how rich solitude—time for yourself—can be. Some have relished in the little things at home, such as finally having the remote to themselves (hurrah!) or being able to listen to the music of their choice. Small, simple things that they hadn't thought of before when a partner was in their company—when they may have had to negotiate, accommodate or say yes when they really meant no. Some have used their newfound alone time to relish in the present moment: to add value, upskill or change something for the better, whether that be themselves, their home or something else in their life. It's a time to take on bigger career opportunities, without anyone holding them back. Or to redecorate or renovate their home, rediscover the joy of reading novels, learn a new language, or even take solo trips to places they'd always dreamed of visiting—solo trips where they can decide the itinerary they want to follow, without compromise, perhaps for the first time in their life. Some of my clients have taken up new hobbies and activities outside of their home, joined local meet-up groups, started lawn bowls or Pilates classes. As a non-runner, I've watched in awe as many people my age have started training for marathons, while I enviously look on. What begins as unfamiliar and strangely quiet territory often transforms into a deeply fulfilling chapter of life, filled with activities that are chosen rather than imposed. The activities you want to do are no longer relegated to 'when I have time' or 'if I have time'; instead, they are a crucial use of your time.

In the time we have alone, in the presence of ourselves, we get a clearer idea of what we want our routine to be, what our priorities are in life, and what boundaries we need to give ourselves and others to allow this life to happen. When we truly relish the present moment, unconcerned about what the world thinks of us, and fully immerse ourselves in the things we have chosen to do, it is a quiet type of delight.

Enjoying time in the present moment, in the now, alone. Who would have thought it?

Motto

 *I will spend time relishing in my presence.* 

Challenge: Five Senses Presence

This is a wonderful mindfulness exercise to help you enjoy the present moment. It's also a helpful grounding technique you can use when you feel anxious or overwhelmed. Start by sitting in a chair either inside your house or, even better, outside in your garden. Keep your eyes open and just sit in the silence for a few moments, sinking into your chair and becoming comfortable. Look around you and bring your attention to five things that you can see in your surroundings. Pick something that you don't normally notice, like a particular leaf on a plant, a small crack in a wall or a cloud in the sky. Then, turn your attention to four things you can hear. Take a moment to listen to your surroundings and note what you are hearing in the background. This may be the buzz of a bee, the hum of the refrigerator or the faint sounds of a lawnmower in your street. Then, notice three things that you can feel or touch. Bring awareness to these three things, such as the texture of your shirt on your skin, the feeling of warmth in your stomach or the comfortable surface of the chair you are sitting on. Now, notice two things you can smell. Turn your awareness to smells that are coming into your nasal passages. Perhaps the breeze is carrying a certain smell from a tree near your home; maybe you can smell the coffee from your freshly made brew or the scent of the body wash from your last shower. Now, bring your attention to one thing you can taste right now, at this present moment. It might be the taste of the last drink you had, or even a hint of toothpaste. Sit there in the comfort of your presence for a little while longer.

This is a quick and relatively easy exercise that can bring your awareness to the current moment and show you how enjoyable and peaceful being present can be. Try spending at least 10 minutes a day doing this exercise.

Chapter 12

Follow Your Inner Compass

At the ripe young age of 23, after completing my university undergraduate studies, I donned a backpack and headed to the UK. It was a trip to visit my English relatives for the first time, but I was also on a one-way plane ticket as I was planning on heading to London to work for a while—and, of course, like many young Aussies, to travel around Europe. After the initial weeks of meeting many of my lovely relatives in northern England (and trying to decipher what on earth they were saying), I got the train down to London. I was totally 'winging it' in terms of where I was going to live and what I was going to do for work, guided only by the 'she'll be right' Australian attitude that would make my present-day organised self shudder. After the initial kerfuffle that ensued after the train doors opened, knocking me onto a train station platform of people moving in a blur, I thought I was well on my way to figuring out what was next. It was mere minutes before it became apparent that my blasé attitude towards living in London had been rather unhelpful, mainly because I didn't know *what actually was next*—namely, where I was going to live and what

I was going to do for work (future organised me would have been rather helpful at that time).

I found a phone booth and called a friend of a friend who was living in London. By chance, she knew someone who could let me stay for one night while I sorted myself out. That night of lying on my jacket in a random person's bed (he was away on a Contiki trip, apparently) turned into two nights, which turned into a week. Before I knew it, I'd upgraded to a bed in a shared room in the house. I was no longer waking up with my jacket buttons pressed into my face; now I had a bed of my own, and it was settling to start to feel a sense of place in this rather large Victorian house in Willesden Green, at least for a few days. It wasn't until then that I realised I was sharing a house with about 12 (give or take) overzealous New Zealanders, something I hadn't thought about in the chaos of the first week when I was in and out trying to sort out accommodation, find a job and nurse an endless hangover.

You'd think being the only Australian in a house full of Kiwis would have meant instant bonding over our shared Antipodean roots, but nope—I was the odd one out, totally 'othered' from the get-go. I said 'feesh and cheeps' instead of 'fish and chips', so of course I sounded like a weirdo to them, and because I had temporarily left a boyfriend back home in Perth and wouldn't partake in any of the shenanigans within the house, I was seen as a bit of a princess (which was probably a fair call, as I still am). We did, however, bond over one situation, when we made it into the London papers a few times. At the time, a local politician was campaigning to rid London of what *The Independent* dubbed 'anti-social, Antipodean and living next door to me'. Our house was targeted as a raucous party house disturbing the neighbourhood, which, as it turned out, happened to be in the same area the politician himself lived in. It became so ridiculous that we were followed by the media whenever we left the house. It was quite exciting; I felt like a celebrity in the mornings, stepping out of my front gate with my handbag held up to my face to walk to the tube station, cameras flashing. I felt quite the rebel, even though I wasn't really involved in anything; I would send the news clippings home to my parents who, I'm sure, were bursting with pride at my rising fame as a public nuisance in London.

Apart from a little bit of bonding over the anti-social Antipodean escapade, I always felt a little odd living there, a little in the minority…but at the same time, quite fine. I'd work all week at my hospital job. On the weekends, I'd get up early, climb over the sleeping bodies strewn all over the house, grab my backpack and go wandering, getting lost on the streets of London. I was happy going off on my own adventure—alone—going wherever I wanted to go, doing whatever I wanted to do, and only stopping to connect with a dear friend of mine from Australia every few weeks, where we laughed, admired good-looking men and ate our way through famous cities. But for the most part, I was able to walk my own path. And it was fabulous. I was completely free from family expectations and away from the shackles of what I *should* be doing—whatever that *should* might have been. I wasn't responsible for anyone or anything. I took spontaneous adventures and had surreal moments when I thought, 'No one on Earth knows where I am right now'. I followed my curiosity through the streets, historic buildings, museums, parklands…way more than I followed any plans. I stumbled upon interesting streets with decaying houses, crumbling graveyards and centuries-old shopfronts. There was an exhilarating kind of anonymity, a freedom to exist without being accountable to anyone. It was liberating to be unattached and unencumbered, and to realise I could steer myself in any direction I chose, wayfaring my own path through life for a while. My housemates were having a great time with themselves (literally), but my inner compass pulled me away from the group I was living with and instead led me down tourist-free cobblestoned streets, where I became lost in places that felt like they belonged only to me, in that moment.

That gap year, of sorts, taught me more than I could have imagined. It was less about ticking off the tourist sites or doing what you're supposed to do as a young traveller in Europe, and more about discovering what it feels like to truly be living on your own terms. As a mental health professional, I think so many people could benefit from an experience like that. I'd love to be able to write a prescription for people that says, 'Take off on an adventure alone and see where it leads you' or 'You don't need these pills; what you need is to just nick off alone for a bit and see how you feel after that'. Maybe it would give them the chance to listen to their own voice, without interruption, and see where it takes them.

Eventually, my little adventure came to an end—probably way too soon, in hindsight—and I returned to Australia, mostly because of the boyfriend I had left behind. But I returned with so much more than memories, and that's because I spent so much time alone, finding my 'self' and getting more clarity around what I wanted to do with my life.

Being alone, at least for a little while, is a chance to discover who you really are outside of everybody else. Who are you without any external expectations placed on you? What really matters to you that is different to what you grew up believing? What do you value and is it different to the other people in your life? Being by yourself gives you a chance to be who you are when no one is watching—and that is because no one is watching! And it allows you to get comfortable with all parts of you, instead of hiding what you think the world needs you to keep hidden. Little moments of aloneness, short periods or long, can give you those moments. When you are alone, you are sensing your way through each day, rather than using a map that has been drawn by someone else. You are intentionally enjoying life in real time and then being guided to listen to and feel whatever you are drawn towards.

Being alone for a while, without anyone else telling you which direction to take or requiring you to compromise, is something all of us should experience, even briefly. Stepping out into the world on your own, immersing yourself in new environments, can help you rediscover who you are (or discover yourself for the very first time).

Putting yourself in unfamiliar situations, meeting new people, trying new activities, making mistakes and even getting completely lost on your own can strengthen your inner ability to navigate life. Over time, these experiences help you build a more trustworthy inner compass—one that guides you toward a more aligned direction.

You don't know what you like or what you don't like until you try it. Being intentionally curious puts you in situations that can awaken what may be dormant inside you, so you can find out what lights you up and see where it takes you. Often, this can only happen when you are *alone*.

Motto

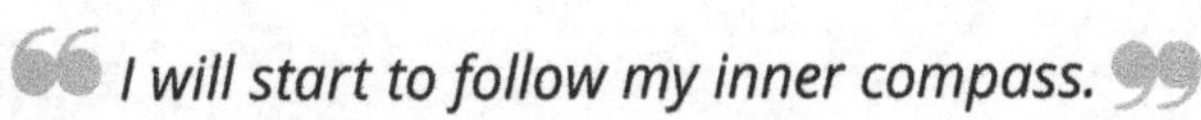

I will start to follow my inner compass.

Challenge: Weekend Solo Trip

We all know that travelling is beneficial for us, but even a weekend away can do us good, particularly when we are alone. Think of a place close by to where you live, maybe an hour or more away — some place you haven't previously spent much time. See if you can book a hotel, motel, or bed and breakfast for at least one night. Apart from accommodation, don't make any plans at all. Take yourself away for that weekend, just you in your car, listening to your favourite music, podcast or book. Once you've checked in to your accommodation, and you've had a little rest, that's when the next part of the adventure starts. Set foot on a walk around the town and just wander, following your curiosity and what piques your interest. For example, is there a bookstore, museum or parkland to explore? Do you want to sit outside a café and just people-watch? Do you want to have long lingering chats to the locals about the history of the town? Be guided by what you want to do, rather than what you feel you should do. Check in with how you are feeling at the end of the trip on the way home.

This is a delightful, if somewhat indulgent, exercise that can really make you reflect on how you truly want to spend your time. You may even realise just how much of your everyday life is shaped by what others want from you. And who knows? You might discover that taking yourself away like this is something you want to do far more often.

Chapter 13

Master Your Mind

I have a pet rainbow lorikeet. I found the feathery ball of bright blue, red and green on the side of the road after he'd been clipped by a car, his wing injured but his feistiness intact. He's aptly named 'The Bird' because I've always aspired to release him back into the wild upon rehabilitation, so I didn't intend to become too attached. However, because of the extent of his injury, The Bird is probably unlikely to ever fly, which means he, and his moods, are likely with me for life. Which is fine by me—and maybe fine by him, depending on said mood. The Bird's day begins when I lift the blanket from around his cage. He wriggles out of his faux fur-lined tent (which he has been sleeping in, on his back with his legs in the air, all night), stretches dramatically with limbs and wings always in the same stretching order, and surveys his cage to see what breakfast is laid out for him. Then comes his fruit platter, his morning bath where he splashes about, and a few rounds of swinging from his ropes. He'll tidy up his tent, removing some fallen feathers from the night, chatter away to the doves who visit, and then, without warning, start acting like a drunken rockstar in a hotel room, trashing his leftovers, hurling his toys and upending pots of food. And, just as quickly, he softens. He might jump on my arm for cuddles, becoming playful and affectionate.

Now, I could talk about my lorikeet all day, as you've probably already gathered. He's not the first of my pets to make an appearance in my books. At this rate, I probably have enough material to fill an encyclopaedia devoted to them all. But here's the thing: when you spend a lot of time alone, small details stand out. The little things become amplified, such as the way a bird stretches in the morning, the way a dog looks at you or the way a cat insists on brushing against your leg. The same goes for evening sunsets, cloud formations in the sky, the shifts of the coastline and the colour of your fussy fiddle-leaf fig's leaves. You just notice more of the little details of your surroundings. But at the same time, the big things—the emotions, the challenges, the silence and the memories—can feel sharper too.

When you're alone, the tiniest details can expand to fill the room, becoming vivid and important in a way they might never be for someone who's got company. A single sound, a single thought, even the way the light shifts through the window, can feel magnified because there's nothing else crowding it out. For someone living with noise and bustle, or who has many people in the house, those same details might barely register. But when you're alone, you quickly learn that your mind needs something to hold on to. Solitude can be nourishing and peaceful, yes. But it can also get really, really quiet. And when it does, if you don't consciously choose where to direct your attention, your mind will happily fill in the gaps for you—at times, rather unhelpfully. And that's the strange thing about attention. What we give it to, and how much space we allow it to take up, can shape the way we experience life.

One of the beautiful things about time alone is that you can spend more time thinking about things but, paradoxically, one of the more awful things about time alone is that you can spend more time thinking about things. This is why it matters that those 'things' are intentional and reasonably positive because, left unchecked, the mind often drifts towards the opposite direction—towards worry, rumination and the ancestral default of scanning for threats. Life will always give us problems to solve, and we need to tune in to those to do something about them. But we have thousands of thoughts a day, most of which are not problems to solve but rather us worrying (living a dress rehearsal in our minds for all the things that could go wrong) or ruminating (replaying thoughts from our past that have already happened). We sit in distress caused by the replaying of accurate or imagined video reels in our mind. I've worked with so many people who, after long stretches of solitude, still circle back to unresolved hurts or replay throwaway comments from others made years ago, amplifying them until they loom far larger than they ever should. To anyone else, those thoughts might seem insignificant against the backdrop of a bigger world. But for the individual, the weight of those thoughts is very real because our perspective narrows when the mind has space to roam unchecked.

Time alone gives you the space and the silence to figure out what's really on your mind. Perhaps something has been on your mind for far longer that it needs to be. With no one there to influence you, and more time in solitude to think, you can start deciphering your worrisome and ruminating thoughts. Some of us may be caught up in thoughts of long ago—replaying a hard conversation from a decade ago, stewing on an old grudge. Others may be dwelling on a traumatic event that they just can't shift. For some, the thoughts replay what's concerning them now—they worry about how they are going to pay the electricity bill, deal with a jerk at work or find the right way to complain to their grumpy neighbour about the broken fence. At other times, the thoughts are imagined, made up of endless possibilities that are likely to not happen: what if I don't see them again, what if it's a disease, what if I don't get asked, what if he gets angry if I speak up, or what if he or she doesn't call? It's an unhelpful trail of 'what ifs' that can spiral you into distress.

For those of us who are prone to unhelpful thinking, as I am, moments of solitude can sometimes feel like a trap. This is why it's so important to learn how to guide your mind before it starts guiding you. Part of this is behavioural—quite literally giving your brain something constructive to do. Feeding it with activities that are enriching, uplifting or practical ensures that your mental energy is being channelled in ways that add value to your life. I'd say I live with a manageable level of anxiety these days, which is a big shift from the high levels I dealt with decades ago. I think that's partly due to the effort I've put in to challenging and reshaping my unhelpful thinking patterns. I also fill my mind, intentionally, with interesting, positive and inspiring things to balance out the more automatic, anxious thoughts that still occasionally show up. It's like I've trained my focus to lean towards what uplifts me rather than what pulls me down. I've also recently stumbled on a wonderful new podcast (new to me, anyway) that I've been enjoying, which has been going for about 16 years, so I have a backlog of over 1600 episodes to listen to. So, even if I stop feeding my mind with all the other fascinating content the world produces, at least I know this podcast is going to keep me going until the next century. Never underestimate the power of distraction to keep your mind engaged and happy.

For other people, being alone with the intention to feed your mind might mean reading an engaging book (good on you for reading this one!), watching a thought-provoking documentary, enrolling in a course or enjoying a hobby that leaves you feeling accomplished rather than depleted. You're adding something to your mind, and your life. That's one of the reasons I have lots of pets. Animals are great for this. By filling the space with positive input, you're less likely to drift into patterns of unhelpful rumination. As human beings, we're natural thinkers (well, most of us are), but when we're left alone with nothing but our thoughts, our thinking activity isn't always helpful. As a mental health professional, I know that if most of us don't give ourselves something to do—if we don't feed our minds with healthy things to think about—guess what? The brain takes over, and you might not like what it gives you to think about.

The other part of mastering your mind involves taking control: becoming skilled at recognising the way you think, noticing if it's unhelpful and then reshaping the way you think so that it is healthier. Being alone can really put a spotlight on unhelpful thinking, which might have been taking control of your thoughts, feelings and behaviours for longer than you can remember. As human beings, we're wired with a negativity bias—a tendency to instinctively focus on what's wrong in our environment, often without even realising it. It's usually the negative aspects that grab our attention first: the problems, the threats, the things that might go wrong. This bias once served our ancestors well. It helped them stay alert, prepare for danger, adapt to change and, ultimately, survive. And while that wiring still has value in today's world, we also need to consciously balance it out. We can do this by deliberately tuning in to the good—training ourselves to notice and appreciate what is going well. This means allowing ourselves to fully experience our positive emotions: letting gratitude, joy, awe and peace linger just a little longer. Being alone gives you the time to train your mind to do this, without the noise of other people. It allows you the quiet moments, the solitude, the stillness to think about how you think, and then mindfully steer your thoughts in a more helpful and healthy direction.

Being thankful, even in the most difficult of times, can make an enormous difference to your mindset and counterbalance the negativity bias—particularly when you are in the depths of despair, when it would be easier, or even more natural, to lose hope. A 2024 meta-analysis by researchers Hittner and Widholm collected 26 studies of gratitude and loneliness involving nearly 10 000 people around the world. Participants averaged 35 years old but largely ranged from college-aged to middle-aged adults. Their results suggest that grateful people tend to be less lonely, no matter their age, gender or where they live. If someone was above average in gratitude, they had a 62 per cent chance of being below average in loneliness. As this is only based on correlational surveys, it's not proven that gratitude reduces loneliness—but the relationship is strong. Incorporating gratitude rituals into your schedule to master your mind is a positive way to steer your mind away from what it will naturally try to focus on—the negative worries about the future or ruminations about the past.

Mastering your mind also means watching for distortions in your thinking and catching yourself when your mind spirals into exaggerations, assumptions or old stories that no longer serve you. Instead of letting those thoughts run unchecked, you can learn to steer them towards perspectives that are more balanced and constructive. Unhelpful thinking styles, also known as cognitive distortions, are irrational patterns of thought that many of us engage in, often without realising. They distort reality by influencing how we perceive situations, which in turn affects how we feel and behave. Many of us are prone to catastrophising (imagining the worst-case scenario), thinking in all-or-nothing terms (ignoring the middle ground), jumping to conclusions (without having all the facts) or even mind-reading (assuming we know what someone else is thinking without any real evidence). I know some people who have been alone for quite a while who get caught in the trap of personalising, believing everything wrong/bad/terrible is because of them—a negative loop of unhelpfulness. One of my clients, Daniel, in our first session together, listed all the things wrong with him, all the things that have happened to him in his life (relationship breakdowns, roofs collapsing, car accidents, redundancies, illnesses, other people's illnesses) and why he was the sole cause of all of it. It obviously wasn't the case, but it took months to rewire his brain not to think like this.

When we are alone, we have the opportunity to look at some of the thoughts that do ticker-tape through the mind. It's a good time to have a think about *how* we think. We can look at the beliefs we have that are unhelpful, redundant or not even ours. Beliefs are thoughts that we think repeatedly, until they become almost solidified in our mind. We form neural connections that are so strong they are part of our physiology (our 'wiring'). These thoughts seem unshakeable until we play around with them a bit, when we may come to the realisation that we, at present, don't 'believe' them anymore. Sometimes we realise the thoughts were never ours to begin with and we just onboarded them from somewhere, at some time, from someone. Sometimes we even realise that they have blocked us in areas of our life, stopping us from doing some of the things that we truly wanted to do. Getting rid of these limiting thoughts and stripping ourselves down to just our own thoughts can not only be cleansing, but it can give us clarity going forward. It's interesting to realise how many of our thoughts are not even our own—they may come from a parent, a teacher, a sibling, an old friend…or an ex. In solitude, you can begin to see these thoughts more clearly, and with that awareness comes the ability to challenge and release them. Instead of being driven by unhelpful ways of thinking, you can feed your mind with nourishing ideas and approach life with curiosity.

When you guide your thoughts in healthy directions, you're literally rewiring your brain—creating new pathways that support growth, resilience and possibility.

Being alone for a while can offer a powerful opportunity to master your mind. It is a chance to observe our thinking, experiment with it and gently guide it towards something more balanced, constructive and kind. This is a helpful thing to conquer, whether we stay alone or embark on relationships with others.

Alone time can literally make you think differently. It's the fertile ground where transformation begins.

Motto

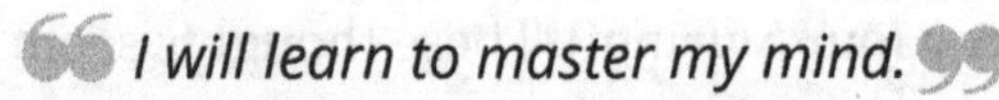

Challenge: Visualise Your Thoughts Passing By

Many of our thoughts are negative, and we can become overly entangled with these thoughts far too often, causing ourselves unnecessary distress. This is called cognitive fusion, as in we 'fuse' with our thoughts, whether they are real or not, often getting ourselves stuck in an unhelpful loop that takes control of our mind. We can become a little more susceptible to this way of thinking when we're by ourselves. Having a mental tool to notice these unhelpful thoughts and move them on is a must if we want to 'defuse' the thought. We want the unhelpful ones to simply pass through our mind.

This week, start to notice your thoughts. Notice whether they carry a positive, negative or neutral reaction from you. Instead of trying to control your thoughts, or even get rid of them, just notice them and let them pass by. It might be helpful to imagine the thoughts like clouds floating by in the sky, or feathers floating down a stream. This can help you allow them to pass through your awareness without giving them undue attention. Then, distract yourself with an activity you know will keep you engaged. Feed your mind with something interesting that lights your mind up, such as reading a book, listening to music or having an interesting conversation with someone.

This exercise is a kind way of letting your unhelpful thoughts pass you by, but also a lovely way to feed your mind with positive things!

Chapter 14

Listen to Your Emotions

It's only relatively recently that one of my clients, Elsie, has finally learned to feel her emotions. Of course, she's been angry and sad, even happy, over the course of her 52 years of life, and able to react at some level to the different events in her life that have required an emotional response. She's laughed a lot, cried when necessary and had her fair share of being annoyed at people. Like many midlifers, she's experienced plenty of emotional events over the course of her adult life, all of which brought with them a host of positive and negative emotions — relationships, relationship breakdowns, marriage, divorce, kids, redundancies, illnesses and deaths. The whole 'adulting' gamut. As she looked back at her life and its series of fortunate and unfortunate events, and the emotions that were attached to said events, she felt 'she had gotten over what she need to get over'. That's why Elsie hadn't even noticed that she hadn't been *feeling* her emotions.

Separated, with her teenagers grown up and spending more time out with their friends, the house was suddenly quieter than it had ever been. She wasn't quite an empty nester as the chicks returned home a few times a day to raid the fridge, but there was a shift in the amount of time Elsie was spending by herself. At first, that silence felt unfamiliar, almost unsettling, but slowly it became a space where long-buried emotions began to stir. There were little moments here and there, when she was going through something at work or dealing with the stress of caring for her elderly parent, when she felt she was sitting in her emotions for longer than she usually did. She said she felt almost 'wallowy'. It was quite an uncomfortable feeling; she was quite proud of the ability she'd had to 'get over it' in the past. This 'wallowy' feeling was concerning her and was the impetus for her to reach out and book a session with me.

For most of her life, Elsie had learned to keep many of her deeper feelings locked away. As a child, Elsie's mother's emotional immaturity had meant her mother's needs had always come first. Her mother wasn't violent or abusive; she was rather emotional a lot of the time herself, expressing the full range of her emotions in a 'reactive' way rather than in a controlled manner. She would yell and scream when she was angry, then lie on Elsie's bed sobbing when she was upset about something. She would burden Elsie with detailed stories that would have been better reserved for adult conversations or even a discussion with a therapist. When Elsie expressed her own feelings of sadness or frustration as a child, she was quickly shut down—told not to be 'so dramatic' or that she was being 'ridiculous'. The message became very clear early on in life: it was safer to be quiet, safer to hold it all in. There was no room for anyone else's emotions in her childhood home, just her mother's.

Like so many of us, she carried that conditioning into adulthood. She was unconsciously drawn towards the familiar, marrying someone whose emotions always took precedence over hers. For years she put herself second, her feelings buried for the sake of harmony. It was better if everyone else was okay. It was easier. She could handle her emotions, but she knew many others couldn't. But unbeknownst to her, decades of holding her emotions back took their toll, not only in her heart but in her body, manifesting as an autoimmune condition that seemed to echo the truth her cells already knew. You can only store so much emotional pain before it begins to find its way out. The body was saying no, when she couldn't.

It wasn't until after her separation, and later as her children grew more independent, that she began to experience little moments of solitude that changed everything. In the stillness, she could finally pause, retrace her past and begin to process what had really happened over the years. Without the constant demands of others, she had found herself thinking, really thinking, about how she felt about her life. For the first time, she had the time and space to stop surviving and start feeling. She could let grief and other stored emotions surface, but also glimpse the possibility of healing. It felt good to be able to really feel, and it was nice to not have to put her feelings on hold (or tuck them away) to cater for everybody else's feelings. She started to express her emotions outwards, rather than internalising them. And she felt so much better for it.

There's something about solitude that invites emotions to surface in ways they rarely do when we are surrounded by others. In the quiet, without the pressure to appear 'fine', grief, sadness, regret and even anger have the space to rise instead of being buried. I've noticed that the more time I spend alone, the more I realise how much I've unconsciously packed away—decades of emotions I never gave myself the time to fully feel. There were big moments in my life that I was simply too busy to process because I was too caught up in my responsibilities, in keeping pace with the world. I was too busy making sure everyone else was okay. My mind must have decided it wasn't the right time, quietly filing those feelings away in a cabinet marked 'later'. But solitude has a way of unlocking that cabinet. In the stillness, without the influence of others or the habit of pushing things down, I find myself able to feel again. I can process and heal in peace.

There are countless moments in life when we feel positive emotions, and just as many when we experience negative ones. As humans, we hold the capacity to feel hundreds of emotions—some of which pass quickly, while others linger and make us uncomfortable. Yet every emotion—yes, even the ones we often label as *negative*—serves a purpose. Imagine our ancestors without fear or anger: would their bodies have been able to prepare them to fight or flee from predators? Or picture them without guilt and shame: would they have been excluded from their tribe, left vulnerable and alone? These emotions, unpleasant as they may feel, were crucial for survival—and in many ways, they still are. Often, the emotions we resist the most are the ones trying the hardest to teach us something.

Life will always present us with difficult emotions. We are such emotionally driven beings that it's easy to let them dominate us. When we allow ourselves to be swept away by negativity, we risk staying stuck on a well-worn path instead of exploring what those feelings are pointing towards. By pausing and really listening to our challenging emotions, we can gather valuable insights about what is and isn't working in our lives. These emotions provide data we can interpret, helping us make better decisions, solve problems and realign our actions with our deeper values and goals. This practice, known as emotional agility, is a helpful skill and allows us to acknowledge how we feel without letting those feelings dictate our behaviour. In doing so, we create space to choose a response that is thoughtful, deliberate and aligned with who we want to be. After all, *irritation* in the moment is human, but allowing ourselves to become an irritated person is optional. *Sadness* in the moment is human, but allowing ourselves to become a sad person is optional.

Loneliness in the moment is human, but allowing ourselves to become a lonely person is optional.

Contentment doesn't come from denying the hard emotions or only chasing the good ones; we achieve contentment by embracing the full spectrum of our emotions. By accepting all our emotions, positive and negative, we cultivate wisdom, resilience and, ultimately, over time, a deeper sense of peace.

You may not have noticed this need to feel all your emotions if not for your time alone.

Motto

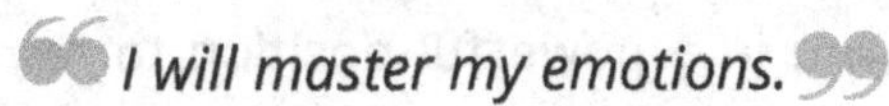

Challenge: Listening to Your Emotions

We are emotionally driven creatures. While this has served our ancestors very well in the past, it can cause trouble for us if we choose to react without thinking first. Ideally, unless we are in a threatening situation, we want to 'respond' thoughtfully rather than 'react' impulsively. It's also important that we don't ignore our emotions, either: whether we feel angry, sad, frustrated, stressed or even lonely, each of these emotions serves a purpose. Ideally, what we want in all situations is to be able to feel our emotions and choose the best behavioural response. So, next time you feel an emotion, stop for a moment and name the emotion you are feeling. Validate your emotion without any judgement, as this emotion is 100 per cent true for you — so allow yourself the space to experience it. Then be curious with your emotion, seeking to understand why you could be feeling this way. Ask yourself: 'Has anything triggered this emotion?' Maybe something has happened in your external environment that has triggered the emotion — for example, perhaps the emotion came over you during a work meeting. If so, what choices will you make to respond to it? Perhaps something internal, like your thoughts, has triggered the emotion — for example, maybe you were thinking about an ex-partner and you began to feel upset. Again, think about the content of the thought, and consider what your options are to solve the problem.

Being able to slow down and *notice* your emotions — naming them, validating them and identifying why you might be feeling them — puts you in a powerful position to *respond* to your emotions, rather than just reacting. This reflective exercise helps you become more aware of your emotions and what they may be trying to tell you. It puts you back in the driver's seat by helping you understand why you feel a certain way, so you can choose how to respond with intention.

Chapter 15
Own Your Inner Strength

Picture this. An attractive naval officer steps out of his car clad in a white naval uniform—white tunic, white trousers, white cap—masculinity personified in a backdrop of grey. He marches through a rustic factory, filled with mostly dishevelled female factory workers. This beacon of manliness turns the head of every female in the room. After passing every production line worker in the factory, he finally lays eyes on the woman he has come to find. He playfully nudges her neck, kisses her passionately, scoops her up in his arms and walks back the length of the factory again. All the while, the female workers stop and clap, with tears running down their faces, proud that she has been rescued. Joe Cocker and Jennifer Warnes croon 'Up Where We Belong' in perfect alignment with our aching hearts, just to double-check our senses are totally fused with the story. He loves her, he chooses her, he saves her. How beautiful. What a happy ending.

This isn't a story from one of my clients in the therapy room, and it most definitely isn't a description of the last date one of my friends went on; instead, it's the rather iconic closing scene of the movie

An Officer and a Gentlemen (sorry, belated spoiler alert), which revolves around the story of a young and handsome member of the US Navy, Zack Mayo (played by Richard Gere) who signs up for aviation training. Along the way he meets the downtrodden and hard-working Paula (played by Debra Winger), who works at the local factory, and an unexpected (but at the same time, expected) romance follows. Twists and turns follow in the story, culminating in an ending fit for a fairytale. This romance rippled through the heart of every woman sitting in a cinema in 1982. The romantic story and the music gave women of the eighties a sensory experience they may not have anticipated—walking out of the cinema with the high hopes and expectations that perhaps they too could have a man as successful and handsome rescue them one day.

Now, I'm not dissing the movie at all. I love it (and yes, I have watched it numerous times). In what is a complete juxtaposition to everything I've said thus far in this book, I'm a hopeless romantic. I know...shock. The thought of looking for love, going out on the prowl and being proactive online (or whatever else people do to hook up these days) positively horrifies me, but romance doesn't. But like many people in midlife right now, I grew up watching an unhealthy amount of unrealistic romance movies in the eighties and nineties. I sometimes catch myself deludedly thinking that the perfect man is going to barge into my lounge room when I'm sitting with my friends and proclaim, 'You complete me', or that he might instead swagger, leather jacket-clad, into the local Chinese restaurant and confidently tell my dad that 'Nobody puts baby in a corner'. Call me romantic, or unrealistic...whatever works for you. I'm a mixed bag of contradictions. Who isn't?

But, in general, I think romance movies of the past really have done us dirty.

I don't think it happens as much anymore; with streaming services available, our diet of entertainment seems to be more wide-ranging, so romances don't tend to dominate as much as they used to. There seem to be more dragons in movies these days. I spent my childhood watching princesses waiting on a prince to either wake them up, give them love's first kiss or return their shoe—all in the guise of being rescued from being alone and figuring things out for themselves. Then I moved straight into my teenage years, when my friends and I ate popcorn and choc bombs while we absorbed stories of how the cute guy rescues the good girl (even with her perm and very big shoulder pads).

So many of us, particularly women, have been conditioned to believe that someone will eventually come along to 'save' us: a partner, a protector, someone who will make everything okay. What we're rarely taught is that we have the capability to save ourselves. We can do hard things. We might not have been exposed to it, we might not think it and we might not have been told it, but we hold within us the psychological strength to endure challenges we never thought possible. It's often only when we're going through something tough, when we're experiencing adversity or even drowning in a life challenge, that we're forced to realise just how resilient we truly are. And with every hard thing we get through, our capacity expands. When we finally understand that we have 100 per cent responsibility for our lives—that our wellbeing and future aren't conditional on anyone else—it becomes one of the most empowering realisations we can ever have. That kind of strength is ours alone, and no one can take it away.

One of my clients, Amber, originally came to see me while she was navigating a challenging separation with her husband. She was working three days a week as a project officer, raising two young boys, and regularly cooking for and visiting her elderly father in aged care. These were just some of the many hats she wore. The mental and physical load had become too heavy, especially after her husband of eight years decided to 'tap out' of the relationship and move on.

As if that wasn't enough, they were right in the middle of home renovations when he left. The back of the house was nothing more than a bare shell, leaving three unfinished rooms with no tiles, no flooring, no paint and no curtains, plus a backyard filled with bright-yellow builder's sand that was perfect for the kids and the dog to run through and bring into the house. Amber wasn't just left with a broken heart; she was also left with the bulk of the parenting, the financial pressure of providing and a half-finished house.

Sitting in the despair of it all, she found herself stuck at first, but then she slipped into solution mode. Over the next six months, she began the journey of rebuilding, literally and figuratively. With the help of YouTube tutorials and a few supportive friends, she learned to lay floorboards, redo a whole backyard with paving, plants and lawn, and even project-manage her mates through the tiling and other fiddly bits she couldn't do herself. When it was finally done, she stood back and felt a deep sense of pride. Before the split, the division of labour had been clear: she managed the inside, and he took care of the outside. But through this experience, Amber discovered a strength she never knew she had—she realised that she could manage *all* of it.

In my time as a therapist, I've seen tremendous growth in clients who've gone through major life disruptions that left them alone and, at least for a while, in a state of despair. But in that aloneness, something remarkable often begins to take shape. People start building capabilities they probably never would have discovered if life hadn't pushed them into solitude. In the mess of it all, they emerge with not only stronger psychological muscles but also a few new practical ones. I've seen people who once swore they'd *never* travel alone now planning regular solo adventures. I've seen gardens ripped out and replaced, and neglected homes transformed one weekend project at a time. Men who had never cooked started making dinner for their kids—sometimes proudly, sometimes chaotically, but always with heart. Women who reluctantly learned to fix blocked plumbing (that may or may not have been me), change flat tyres and tackle car repairs with YouTube as their co-pilot (also me). I've watched clients climb ladders to fix leaking roofs, paint entire rooms or set up their own businesses from scratch—all things they'd once thought they couldn't do. Because when you're alone, there's no one else to outsource life to. And in the doing, in the small, gritty acts of keeping yourself and your world together, resilience quietly takes root.

I often encourage my clients, especially in their low moments, to look back across their lives so far. Often they see challenges that, in the moment, they'd never believed they'd overcome, like a divorce, the death of a parent, an illness, bullying at work or the breakdown of a relationship. Such life events are never on the wish list, and we deludedly think we will never experience them...until they happen. I remind them that those same strengths, those same inner resources that they drew on or developed at those times, are still within them and can be tapped into to help them navigate whatever they are facing today.

When it comes to being alone, most of us don't realise what we're capable of until we have no choice but to find out. In the past, we've had others to lean on—people to share the load, step in when things get hard or take care of the stuff we don't want to face. But when you're on your own, it all lands squarely on your shoulders. There's no one to cry to at the end of the day, no one to fix the leaking tap, no one to put the spider outside or wrestle with the jam jar. When the car breaks down, when the pet must be put to sleep, when the kids are sick in the middle of the night…you are it. You don't get to handball it to anyone else. Sometimes you bumble your way through, sometimes you fall apart in the middle of it but, one way or another, you get it done. You learn to rely on yourself, and you realise, over time, how strong you are.

We hear the word resilience tossed around a lot these days, so much so that some people have grown to dislike it, seeing it as a buzzword used to gloss over deeper, systemic issues, as if people just need to toughen up, stay stoic or put up with things they shouldn't. It's as though being more 'resilient' will help all tough situations, like waving a magic wand over something challenging. There are workshops on it, experts preaching it and a philosophy that if only we could master it, life would somehow be easier. But it doesn't really work like that. You can't simply learn resilience by reading about it or attending a seminar. Resilience isn't theoretical; it's lived. To be resilient, you must go through something hard. You must be in the trenches, face the discomfort, be squeezed by the weight of it all—almost wrung out, like a cloth—and somehow survive it. You must go through it all, fall on the floor, lay there a while, dust yourself off and then get up again. Then, one day, you will look back and think, 'Wow, I didn't think I'd get through that'—and yet you did.

And that's when the magic of resilience really shows itself. The next time you face something tough, your brain draws on what it's already learned. It applies a familiar formula, tapping into those psychological capabilities you've developed, or perhaps discovered, before.

That's the quiet strength of resilience. It's not taught in a classroom; it's built through living. And it develops considerably when you're alone.

Motto

*I will recognise the strength that resides inside of me.*

Challenge: Reflective Life Review

We often look back at our life and remember the best moments — and, of course, the more challenging moments — with memories attached that elicit a heightened state of emotion that we can often feel to this day. But in many cases, we don't think too much about the growth that happened for us in those tough times, nor the psychological capabilities that became stronger through that struggle. Taking time to thoughtfully revisit the significant events in your life, ranging from childhood to the present, is a great way to internalise how strong you are. Take out a notebook and recall and write down challenging situations in your past, pausing to observe what happened, and then identify the strengths you demonstrated during those times. For example, you might note down resilience, adaptability, empathy, resourcefulness, being hard-working or even perseverance as key strengths you developed during those times. Thinking through these inner strengths, and owning them, can help build your confidence in your abilities to get through struggles in the present moment, and in the future. This activity is a reflective chance to see all that you've gone through, and how much growth you have achieved — all of which will help you going forward.

Chapter 16
Tap into Your Creativity

I was never a diary keeper as a child. I mean, my parents gifted me a diary every year at Christmas, and I 'kept' it: one of those colourful diaries with a silver key attached at the side that you could cut off and hide separately in your sock drawer, away from your most annoying sibling and their snooping ways. That flimsy little key was supposed to give us a (false) sense of security that our secrets would be kept safe and intact.

Flicking through my new diary each year, with its crisp white blank pages, I was always excited about what the year would bring. I had all good intentions of penning Adrian Mole-style accounts of my teenage experiences: my deepest, darkest thoughts and musings about the incoming year. It would be an accurate record of my childhood that I knew future me would find valuable. But the day-to-day reflective record of my childhood and teenage years never eventuated. Alas, I obviously became busy doing other things, and like many a fancy notebook, those diaries were relegated to the bottom drawer and, in my later high school years, became just a reminder of when my assignments were due.

Except in 1991. For some reason, 1991 was heavenly chosen as the one year of my whole life I would keep a diary. I hadn't written one before, and I haven't written one since, but I have one full diary from 1991. And it's glorious. Page by page filled up with words, pictures, love hearts (lot of love hearts) and loose printed photos with classmates' faces scribbled out. One whole high school year of highs and lows, captured in pure adolescent fine detail. Ending on 31 December 1991 with the profound entry, 'Last day of the year. Going out for dinner. Hope 1992 is a better year. Seeya'. And since 1991, this diary has been kept in a hat box filled with other nineties paraphernalia—a pile of *TV Hits* magazine Celebrity Swap cards; Milli Vanilli, Paula Abdul and New Kids on the Block music lyrics cards; and—weirdly, stalker-like—a crush of mine's orange sports shirt.

As far as deep reflections or musings go…well, there doesn't seem to have been much of any of that. It was a (very) simple account of my day-to-day happenings: this happened, that happened, I like this, I don't like that, who was annoying, how mean my mum was that day, what crush I had walked past…and the rest of it was just reflections on what sucked. Interestingly, 1991 was the year that Pop passed away (remember Pop from Chapter 6?), so the tone in my diary pages shifts somewhat, from shallow teenage perceptions to something a lot deeper—words wrapped in sadness, with my entries more thoughtful and emotional around those weeks.

Flicking through those pages now, what I notice about 1991 is that there was so much creativity. Lots of imagining, dreaming and designing, actualised as drawings, writing, poetry, collages of pictures and swirling handwriting styles, with the stroke of the last letter having a cute serif tailing off it. Always. It's a form of creativity that I don't remember happening outside of my diary;

it seems I reserved it for myself, in those pages. My elaborate handwriting looked in the style of a forlorn Victorian soldier writing to his beloved about how he longed for her and feared he wouldn't get the chance to hold her again.

It is an interesting read, that diary. Lots of teenage angst: I wish he noticed me, I wish I was prettier, she isn't speaking to me, how embarrassing, I'm worried, I hate school … the usual. But one of the most interesting things is to read what I left behind that year, and to realise which direction I headed in once that diary year had finished. I was halfway through high school in 1991, and at that turning point where teenagers are told to make big decisions about their life. We're guided to start fine-tuning our subject choices to pursue certain pathways, as if most of us had any clarity around this. Making big calls, at the wise old age of 15, about what we wanted to do for the rest of our lives. Although she didn't write about it, 1991 me had obviously decided that it was best to step away from all things creative and move in an entirely different direction. Her thought process, or lack thereof, determined what I do as a career as an adult, and what I am still doing to this day. A dimming of my creativity ensued and continued to lay dormant for many, many years.

As a child, I spent a lot of time in my own company, simply because I liked it. Being an otrovert (refer to Chapter 5 for more on this), it's in my nature to enjoy solitude; I never felt the need to seek out groups, preferring instead to be entertained by my own thoughts and the freedom of following my mind wherever it wanted to go. But, like many people, as I moved through my teens and into adulthood, my life expanded — relationships, socialising, parenting — and with that came more people, more noise, more demands. All these things are wonderful in their own ways, yet they also bring expectations and less space for solitude. Over time, the outside world can quietly dim who you once were, what you once thought, what you once believed in and what you truly wanted to be spending your time doing. Being alone again gives you some of those moments back. It gives you the chance to step back from some of the people who've unwittingly contributed to the dimming of your self. It gives you the time to think separately from everyone else, find your own answers and start designing your life in a way that feels true to you.

Being alone for a little while, without as much input from the outside, can give your imagination the space to start lighting up again. Yes, it might start off as being creative to keep yourself busy. Just look at people's behaviours during the pandemic. Forced into lockdown, disconnected from the outside world and feeling scared and uncertain, people filled their time with baking, painting, knitting, jigsaw puzzles... anything to distract their mind from worry and attempt to inject some happiness into their lives. But what also happened is that they tapped into a creative streak inside themselves that may have been long forgotten, pushed so deep inside that they had forgotten it existed. It had been crushed under all the roles, responsibilities and endless to-do lists, many imposed by others. Spending time creating slowed people down, de-stressed them and made them realise that they were, indeed, creative. That they *could* create. And without the global crisis of the pandemic, this realisation might not have happened if the status quo had remained intact. Sometimes it's not until we are thrust (or kicked) out of our comfort zones that we realise what capabilities we have. And for many creatives, they need the alone time first to remember that.

What comes to mind when you think of a creative? You might conjure up the image of a loner or someone who works in solitude. Perhaps they are a scruffy musician strumming their guitar alone in their garage, an artist painting a portrait in a studio or a writer sitting at a typewriter in their study overlooking a lake (why do I always visualise a writer typing on a vintage typewriter?). Whatever or whoever comes to mind, they are usually alone. While being alone is by no means the only way to create, it certainly is something that many creatives talk about requiring to get the creative juices flowing. It is in silence where the muse makes the appearance.

Many elderly folks take up creative tasks when they are alone and, once again, have more time. They crochet, start gardening and may even learn an instrument. But why should we wait until we are older to do this? Having moments of alone time earlier on in our lives is a chance to try out new things to see if we enjoy them, maybe even to see if we're good at them or we feel they could be good for us. These are things that we want to do for no other reason than because we want to. Perhaps, in taking this time, we might find out something about ourselves that we never knew. We might discover we have a talent that we had never given a chance. We might just love doing something that we didn't know we loved before. We might start creating things that we didn't think were ever possible, our imagination lighting up with ideas, inspiration and innovation.

Most creatives talk about the importance of alone time, saying it's necessary for creation. Without it, many pieces of art may not have been developed. Solitude is where creatives get the time for mental wandering, experimenting with new ideas and trying out new things without the interference of others. In other words, they block out the external world and retreat inwards, and they are then compelled by what is coming from inside. Creativity seems to come easily when we're able to utilise the parts of our brain that are less connected to reality and more free-flowing. We've all felt that 'aha' feeling when our brain wanders. The time to separate your thoughts from the collective, allow space for new ideas to sprout and reflect in silence is something money just can't buy. The best ideas I've ever had have not come from sitting in a boardroom with others, nor from being on a conference call. My best ideas come to me when I am walking my dog out in nature somewhere (always when I'm trying not to work or be creative). Even in the shower. How many of us have succumbed to 'the shower effect'? Attempting to solve a personal issue by thinking about it or staring at our computer until we find the solution to a work problem rarely works, and yet when the answer finally comes it arrives while we are alone in the shower, doing something routine and not 'thinking' anymore. The brain's executive functions are having a bit of a rest from the daily overwhelm and allowing our mind to just pause and wander, giving it space to come up with solutions, answers and ideas without the external pressure that we get so used to. All it takes is for us to be alone, with the mind at ease while we feel a little less stressed, to come up with the goods.

But isn't this all of us? Aren't we all creatives? Every moment, we are in the process of creating our days, our weeks, our years. Whether you believe you are creating solo or co-creating with another entity—a god, the universe or even your higher self—you are still creating. You are creating your life. We are creating whether we like it or not. We express ourselves through art. The art we are designing is our life.

Being alone for a while gives you precious time free from the noise and demands of the outside world. It's in that stillness that imagination begins to stir and the gold hidden within the mind starts to surface. Beneath all the clutter and expectations that we absorb from the world around us lies a rich inner landscape waiting to be explored. You don't have to be painting, writing poetry or making music (although this is all very lovely). Time alone could give you the time to create what's next for *you*. Design the life that you truly want. Imagine what you want for yourself. Think of ideas to try. Make mistakes and scribble over them.

It's in the quiet moments of simply *being*, rather than constantly *doing*—in the moments when you are away from outside influences—that your brain truly lights up and creativity has the space to breathe. This seems to happen more often when you are alone.

Motto

 *In my time alone, I will tap into my creativity.* 

Challenge: Adding a Play Ritual

Play is not just for children; it's also important for adults. Incorporating playful activities into life can have numerous benefits for creativity and overall wellbeing. However, it's sometimes hard to work 'on' our life, while we are busy 'in' it. Many of us find ourselves caught up in the responsibilities of our work and daily routines, doing the same thing every day and forgetting the importance of fun activities.

Think about a creative activity or two that you could ritualise into your weekly regime — it needs to be something other than what you do for work. It might be painting, drawing, cooking a new recipe, dancing, knitting, pottery, playing an instrument or even creating a herb garden. It might even be sitting with a bowl of popcorn and watching an old rom com that you know you love. Spend some time each week (or even each day) mindfully engaging in this activity, for no other reason than to enjoy it. Ritualise it into your schedule as though it is as important as all the other tasks and duties you do. After a few weeks, notice how you feel and see if any new ideas for your life have entered your mind as a result. It's a lovely (and fun) way of spending time in the moment, knowing that you are doing it just for the pure enjoyment.

Chapter 17

Nurture Your Relationships

Back in my university days, when I was running on information overload, sheer exhaustion and way too many bad coffees, I remember sitting in a lecture after yet another sleepless night of assignments. A few of us students (postgraduates, mind you), who had become good friends, were slumped together in our seats, bleary-eyed and chatting away about our common study woes, when a guest lecturer quietly walked in, his trousers hitched way too high (apparently for my liking that day, at least).

I'm pretty sure I was the first to crack, letting out a tiny, muffled sound that was the beginning of a laugh while also trying to look down and distract myself from it, obviously knowing that letting the laugh out would be extremely unprofessional and totally uncalled for. Then I smiled and a little bit more of a silent laugh came out, but I was able to halt it. I flicked through the papers in my lever-arch file and rustled through my pencil case searching for a pen I didn't need—anything to steer my mind elsewhere. But of course, holding it in only made things worse (a bit like 'holding in a sneeze' energy … *it's not possible*).

Instead of just smiling, my shoulders started shaking, which set off my friend sitting next to me. Which then set off the friend sitting next to her. Before long, all of us were caught in a wave of uncontrollable giggles, doing everything and anything that we could to try and distract ourselves so we could stop. It was so bad. The harder we tried to stop, the worse it got; one person would calm down, only for someone else to snort and send us all off again. The laughter continued way past what had initially instigated it. Eventually, it got so bad that the lecturer *walked out* of the lecture theatre, leaving us all sitting there. To this day, I still think it's the worst thing I've ever done as a human being, but we simply couldn't control the emotional contagion once it took hold. Later that day, I took it upon myself to apologise to him, stumbling through an explanation about being delirious from lack of sleep and assuring him our outburst had nothing to do with him (which was only half true).

Most of the funniest moments I've had in my life have been with my friends, whether it's inappropriate giggle outbursts, playful banter, inside jokes or even just shared nostalgic stories where we are laughing with each other (and *at* each other). That's not to say my romantic relationships haven't had entertaining moments, of course they have, but there is something extra special about the hilarity and bonding that happens when there is a group of friends laughing together, whatever age you are at the time. I have early memories of sitting in a row with my friends in primary school, when my friends fell backwards off their chairs, desperately grabbing at the trays under their desks, only to bring the entire contents (pencil shavings and all) crashing down on top of them. Then there are the funny shared moments in the workplace, like dealing with the same difficult customer, repeatedly, while a work friend sat beside me struggling to keep a straight face. Or the time I was driving with my mate and the gear stick on my Datsun 120Y snapped clean off mid-drive, leaving us in disbelief as we just rolled, gear-less, down the hill, drowning in uncontrollable laughter. And the pièce de résistance of comical friendship moments, the one that completely broke me, happened during an innocent little playdate at my house with a fellow mum. Her little boy toddled over to us on the couch, all cuteness and pride, and as politely as if he were handing his mum a piece of cake, placed into her hand something he'd just pulled out of his nappy. Let's just say … it was not a brownie.

I recently spent a few days down south with a group of girlfriends, and my face was sore from laughing. We bonded over beautiful food, long bush walks, vulnerable conversations and some very, very entertaining stories. Though now, as a midlifer, the giggles tend to hit a little differently because, let's be honest, there's always the risk of wetting yourself. One should always be a little nervous about laughing too hard when you pass through and beyond middle age. But then again, we'd support each other if it happened.

Apart from being a great source of smiles, playfulness and laughter, friendships are one of the greatest sources of certainty and stability we have, running in parallel to the more unpredictable flow of our romantic relationships. Relationships with our partners may come and go, but friendships often anchor us through life's changes. Yes, I know they sometimes do swap and change a little, but there's usually a little pack of people that we like and who we can rely on outside of romance. Some people jump on our 'social' bus early on in our life journey, becoming friends at an early age — maybe from the neighbourhood, a school, a first job or a sport. Some stay on for the full ride, while others get off and take another bus in an entirely different direction, never to be seen again. Others join us and disembark at different points along the way, hopping on and off during the various phases of our lives — through education, jobs, travel, relationships, volunteer roles or mutual friends. I've even made friendships while out walking my dog, bonding over whether I found the owner of that stray tabby, what's with all the roadworks and how stormy the weather has been of late. This kind of small talk assists us in knowing that we can take the conversation a little deeper the next time we say hello.

For a variety of reasons, some of which can cause emotional turmoil, friendships fall away over time. In a world that feels busier and more fragmented than ever, it's not uncommon for friendships to drop away through no fault of anyone: our lives shift, our priorities change and sometimes we move on. As children, friendships feel more effortless, but as adults, we become more guarded, often neglecting our social life while our careers, relationships, children and other responsibilities take over. I've had many friendships that have unfortunately subsided over time, through no fault of anyone but as a result of the tides of a busy adulthood.

Deep, genuine connections are critical to our wellbeing. These social relationships give us a feeling of belonging: someone to debrief with, learn from and lean on, physically and emotionally. Strong friendships have even been linked to lower anxiety and depression, better immunity, faster recovery from illness and longer life expectancy. And while about one-third of Australians today report feeling lonely, this isn't always about a lack of company. Often, it's emotional loneliness, the absence of close, soul-level connection. Many of the world's ills have been blamed on other things, but the fact that it's disconnection that is causing them is rarely discussed. Loneliness is not necessarily about having no people around; instead, it's when we're not connecting with the people around us. It's about not being able to share parts of ourselves with others—not being able to share the highs and lows, the good and the bad, the successes and the failures, and the light and the dark with someone who just 'gets' us.

Relationships need to be nurtured; they need time and effort. Since 1938, the Harvard Study of Adult Development has been investigating what makes people flourish in the longest in-depth longitudinal study on human life ever undertaken. After starting with 724 participants, including boys from disadvantaged and troubled families in Boston and Harvard undergraduates, the study incorporated the spouses of the original men and, more recently, more than 1300 descendants of the initial group. Across the course of time, researchers were able to watch participants living through the trials and tribulations of life, falling in and out of relationships, finding success and failure at their jobs, and having families, as well as experiencing other life events: the usual life trajectory. The study's simple conclusion is that 'good relationships lead to health and happiness' but 'the trick is that those relationships must be nurtured'. In his now-famous TEDx talk, the study's director, Dr Robert Waldinger, stated, 'Our study has shown that the people who fared the best were the people who leaned into relationships, with family, with friends, with community'.

It may seem a bit of a paradox, but time alone without a partner can make you better at social relationships. One obvious reason for this that comes to mind is that without a partner, people often have more time to spend with their friends. Research has shown that couples tend to spend most of their time with their partner and accidentally leave their friendships behind. A 2015 article by Sarkisian and Gerstel in the *Journal of Social and Personal Relationships* found that being single increases the social connections in the lives of both men and women, noting that there are social constraints associated with marriage. In 2012, researchers Musick and Bumpass reported in the *Journal of Marriage and Family* that partners were asked over the course of six years to describe the quality of the relationships they have with their friends and family, as well as the frequency of meetings. The research found no evidence that marriage and cohabitation provided benefits over being single in the realm of social ties and that entering a partnership reduced contact with friends. It's not surprising that forming a co-residential relationship reduces time with others, as partners spend time together that cannot be spent elsewhere. Interestingly, the withdrawal from friends, family and others was the same for those cohabiting with their partners *regardless* of the duration of the relationship. The catch-cry of the busy adult in a relationship is often 'we must catch up soon' with no actual follow up, with partners just doing the 'right thing' by their partners, but unfortunately a by-product is having less time to nurture those friendships. So, being alone for a little while might give you back some time to spend with those mates.

Spending time alone can also give you clarity about which friends are beneficial in your life and how you deserve to be treated. Once you've spent more time alone and become more accustomed to it (like when you start feeling content in your own company), you notice who, socially, is good for you. Spending time alone can help you cultivate your own energy, rather than constantly reacting to the energy of others. When you're truly comfortable in your own company—when your thoughts are calm and grounded—it can feel like living in a self-sustaining ecosystem. There's peace in that independence. Then, when you step out of that space to spend time with others, something interesting happens: it becomes much clearer who adds to your life. You can feel it; maybe you're more inspired and more energised, or you feel lighter, heard or simply more joyful after being with certain people. And, of course, the opposite can be true too. We can walk away from certain social interactions feeling lower in mood, heavier, unheard, confused and sometimes even quite bad about ourselves. Solitude sharpens that awareness and can lead you to being more intentional about who you share your time and energy with, not because you're isolating but because you've realised that being alone is not lonely: it's *enough*. And when being with someone feels even better than being alone, that's a sign they're worth your time. Gradually, it becomes more obvious who you want in your life and who you don't, rendering you a little choosier about who you spend time with. One of the unexpected gifts of being alone is that you refine your choices about the people you spend time with, and you will enjoy times with friends more when they are better for your wellbeing.

When we have spent time alone, we have had time to be ourselves, without putting on a façade or shapeshifting for different people (which is exhausting, and yet something that many of us do way too often). When we 'shapeshift' in this way, we are almost morphing into the people we're surrounded by and conforming to their interests, beliefs, values and so on (for survival reasons), which means we may lose our own sense of self. The more time you spend being authentic and real, the more likely you are to find your tribe and connect with people like you.

In my teenage years and early adulthood, I really didn't question whether I needed a partner. There was no self-inquiry at all. It never occurred to me that perhaps I should be by myself for a while. I just unconsciously followed a pathway that involved looking for love, never stopping to think that some alone time might do me some good. The friends that I had seemed to be just like me: we had crushes, boyfriends and flings, peppered with some unrequited love stories, until we ended up in a long-term relationship. Society didn't tell us that love and connection can come from so many others beyond a partner. Statistically, many of us will unfortunately lose a partner at some point, so it's important that we don't put all our eggs in the basket labelled 'romantic relationship'. Even when we stay with one partner forever, they shouldn't be responsible for everything. We need to form connections within a whole village—not just with one person.

When we give ourselves a little more time on our own, consciously boosting our social relationships is a must because connection is important too. We need to put in the effort to nurture current friends and be open to finding new ones. Sometimes friendships develop organically—we just gel with someone at work or meet someone out networking who laughs at our jokes. You just 'know', so you make plans to see each other again, liking and trusting them enough to take the friendship further away from its original context. Other times, proactively becoming more social requires intention and openness, which is something that many adults feel quite socially anxious about. It takes time to get to know, like and trust new people, so we may also need to be patient—otherwise we might not give people enough of a chance before we run away from them. Some people may also feel uncomfortable with opening their lives to new people. In this case, focus on engaging in new hobbies and activities, or becoming involved in causes you genuinely enjoy, just for the sake of it, without the pressure to mingle, as you may see a friendship develop as a bonus.

Sometimes the best people to spend time with are the low-hanging fruit—the people who are there, right in front of us, but we got too busy to notice. Think back to the people in the past who you once bonded with or laughed with and reach out to them. Contact the people who make you feel good when you are around them—those who make you smile.

Being alone can also improve many other relationships, apart from friendships. Many people without partners have their children to themselves more, so time at home that would usually be spent with a partner can be spent with the children. Longer conversations about their day (this may or may not occur with teenagers but see how you go!), time to go out for lunch or time to spend watching a movie is valuable bonding time. You can also make more time for other family members. Many people still have elderly parents that need time and support. That alone time gives you back the time to spend with them, rather than rushing off to be with your partner. Our parents are not here forever, and so a little more time with them might be something you, and also them, would value.

Finally, the foundation of any future romantic relationship is a friendship. Taking the time to deeply know someone, to connect with someone, to be friends with someone before going any further is a worthwhile plan if you are to start dating again. Give yourself the time to get to really know someone before jumping into something too quickly. You can build a deep friendship that may (or may not) develop into a relationship. We rarely move from zero to one hundred with friends. We don't lock them in forever or move them into our house quickly, like we tend to do in romantic relationships. Keeping the brakes on while you nurture other areas of your life as your relationship builds is a healthier way to embark on something new.

Sharing ourselves with others is better for everyone, and connecting to others is crucial when you're alone.

Motto

Challenge: Nurturing Friendships

So many social relationships can fall by the wayside as adults. We get busy, we get distracted and we tend to presume that everyone is like this, so we don't contact people. Many adults feel lonely and wish that someone would reach out and contact them (I hear this _all_ the time!). So, get out your mobile phone and look at your contact list. Scroll through the names and see which ones light you up — whether you have seen them recently or not. They may be current friends, friends from the past, colleagues or even acquaintances. Make note of who these people are. You might even want to do this with your connections via a social media account — whichever one that more of your friends from now and the past are engaging with. Make a note of any people on the list whose name makes you smile. Now, spend some time reaching out to these people. It might be a quick check-in to see how they are; it might be sending them a funny meme that you know they would resonate with; it also might be a 'Hey do you want to organise a catch up soon? I'd love to see you' type of message. Send anything you know would be beneficial to nurture the friendship. Yes, many adults are busy, but they will like to know that you are thinking of them too. You never know, a beautiful friendship could come out of it!

Chapter 18
Self-Compassion for Your Lonely

'That's the most ridiculous thing I've ever heard', snorted my old school friend recently when we caught up for our twice-yearly lunch—something we've partaken in since high school finished. Not one to mince words, it was still a carefully chosen response, after patiently listening to me rattle off a lengthy list of reasons as to why I haven't dated anyone since she saw me last (a list she's heard come out of my mouth numerous times).

'Well, I'm not setting you up anymore anyway. Remember that last one…you're an idiot', she added, shaking her head playfully and then turning her attention to her ricotta gnocchi. She was referring to the fact that I didn't give a rather charming and successful friend of hers a chance. It had been *more than 10 years ago*.

'He's happily married now, so it all turned out the way it was supposed to', I said with a guilty chirp, before swiftly changing the topic to something other than my relationship status.

Across the course of my life, I've had various relationship statuses. Of course, there's the 'totally-in-love-with-celebrities' phase that went on in the pre-teen years, when I had Tom Cruise, Patrick Swayze and Rob Lowe collaged across every piece of wall in my bedroom, preoccupying not only my mind but my heart. Then, as I entered my teenage years, I moved on to crushes with real people (albeit not always reciprocated) and eventually became someone's long-term girlfriend. As an adult, I've been a single woman living on her own, coupled up, married and, once children came along, married with children. I've then been separated with children; I've been dating on occasion; and I've been a solo parent sans dating. Throughout all of that, I've had many moments of being alone and many moments of feeling lonely. But, looking back, I realise that those moments of loneliness were never really about my relationship status or who I was with at the time. They were about connection, or a lack of it. The loneliest moments weren't the times I was physically alone; they were the times I was in unhappy relationships, stuck in limbo with someone I no longer felt connected to and feeling as if I had nowhere to go. Looking back, those were also the times when I was totally out of alignment with my 'self'.

Thinking about my life, I didn't feel lonely as a small child playing with my pets, or as a teenager while sitting in my room listening to Madonna cassettes and singing into my hairbrush in front of the mirror. I didn't feel lonely as a student when I was holed up in my study drowning in research articles and writing my doctoral thesis. I didn't feel lonely as a young woman wandering the cobblestoned streets of London, stepping into old bookstores and browsing with a cappuccino in my hand. I didn't feel lonely taking yoga classes as a separated woman. I didn't feel lonely starting a business on my own as a single parent.

Even now, without a partner, I don't feel lonely when I'm at home with my children. I don't feel lonely when I'm taking long lingering walks around the river with my dog and I don't feel lonely when I'm lying on the couch engrossed in a book. I don't feel lonely when I'm laughing with my girlfriends over wine and cheese, and I don't feel lonely when I'm conjuring up new business ideas in my mind. I don't feel lonely when I'm concocting new salad recipes, and I certainly don't feel lonely when I'm writing (phew, because that would be a lot of lonely).

But in some relationships, I did feel lonely when my partner was lying to me, hiding the truth or trying to control me. I did feel lonely when there was emotional disconnection and I was wondering why. I did feel lonely when I had to hide my own true feelings or couldn't speak up to avoid conflict. I did feel lonely when the relationship was totally consumed by and about the other person. I did feel lonely when I was putting up with downright awful behaviours. I did feel lonely when we were growing apart, and I did feel lonely when I abandoned parts of myself to be with that person.

I felt lonely when there was a disconnection within my self: a disconnection, a misalignment, a deep knowing that what was happening wasn't right…*for me*.

But my lonely, and your lonely, will be different to other people's lonely. I've worked with people who feel lonely when their partner doesn't listen—they aren't hearing or validating how they are feeling. People who feel lonely because every night their partner spends more time staring at a screen than them. People who feel lonely because they are constantly walking on eggshells and have to dance around certain topics of conversation. People who feel lonely when their partner withdraws from them, when they are taken for granted or even when their conversations are just about the surface-level practicalities of life and nothing deeper (Who's cooking dinner? Has that bill been paid? Who is picking the kids up?). Some people feel lonely because they do the lion's share of the work in the house, and others feel lonely because they are just plain treated like shit. And many, many of my clients feel lonely because they feel as if they are living with a roommate rather than a partner—someone they're bound to on paper and yet feel completely disconnected from. A once-natural connection has become a forced coexistence.

To add to the wound of a relationship that isn't working—when people stay disconnected within it, feigning connection while nothing changes—the loneliness continues, along with the disconnection to the self, leading people to become a person they are not supposed to be.

Of course, what I've mentioned throughout this book doesn't cover the full spectrum of being alone by any stretch. Because throughout life, inevitably, the risk is that we *will* find ourselves alone at some point. We may not always feel a physical distance, but we will feel disconnected from others, misunderstood, unheard, out of sync with the crowd, or at odds with what others think or value at certain times in our lives. But it's not the loneliness itself that matters: it's what you do with it that counts. There will be times when it's just you, and only you. In those moments, you must learn to be your own best friend—to be your own partner.

Don't compare your lonely to someone else's lonely. It's *your* lonely. If you're feeling it, that's the signal to turn inwards with kindness and be there for yourself. You shouldn't feel guilty or ashamed for feeling lonely. It's normal. If you do feel like this at times, offer yourself some self-compassion and be there for your *self*.

Self-compassion refers to how we relate to ourselves when we're going through something challenging in life. It involves being warm and caring with ourselves, while also leaning in to help and offering support—just like we do when we are showing compassion to other people. We are stepping in to connect, rather than stepping away from them. As self-compassion expert Kristin Neff explains in a 2023 *Annual Review of Psychology* article:

> The experience of compassion is similar when applied to our own suffering, whether it stems from failure, feelings of personal inadequacy, or life challenges more generally. It involves being present with our own pain, feeling connected to others who are also suffering, and understanding and supporting ourselves through difficult moments.

When you feel lonely, treating yourself like you would your best friend is a helpful place to start. We are always our wisest self and peak sage when we are giving advice to others (like me talking to you now). When our friends are going through a challenging time, we feel the pain along with them. We call them, we sit with them, we validate them. We ask questions and wonder alongside them. We seek to understand what the pain is all about, and we seek to soothe them. We work with them to figure out what they need to ease the pain. We give them hugs and send sarcastic memes that relate to the experience they are going through. It's empathy in action, whereby we feel alongside them but can also help to do something about the situation. For some, their lonely needs a big tub of cookies and cream ice-cream and some laughter with their mates. For others, their lonely needs silence, needs to run, needs to cry or just needs some time. When loneliness shows up, don't run away from it. You've got to sit with your lonely with compassion, and it will eventually tell you what it needs.

It's not the loneliness that matters, it's what you do with it that counts. What's yours telling you?

Motto

 *I will practice self-compassion daily.* 

Challenge: Self-Compassion Journal Writing

One way to release bottled up, uncomfortable emotions and unhelpful thoughts is to boost self-compassion by writing in a journal. Journal writing is a wonderful way to release whatever is on your mind: feelings, worries, ruminations, stories and anything else that gets you stuck at times! Journal writing helps with the processing of emotions; it can help you identify some unhelpful thinking patterns and allow you to have some powerful realisations over time. It's very cathartic!

You don't have to follow a specific format to benefit from this practice. You can just write the words that pour out of your mind in any way they come out. No need to edit! But to boost the self-compassion, it might be nice to end your journal entry with some of these prompts:

> ➤ 'One of my wins today was ...'
> ➤ 'I'm proud of myself for ...'
> ➤ 'An area where I've shown a lot of growth is ...'
> ➤ 'Compared to this time last year, I'm doing a lot better with ...'
> ➤ 'One way I could show myself more compassion is ...'

Try writing in your journal at the end of each day, and over time notice how your mind and body respond.

Chapter 19
Discover Your True Self

When I first met Brent, he was only 23 and still living at home with his parents. A clever, bookish young man, he would literally lug around a copy of Leo Tolstoy's *War and Peace* and balance a large cappuccino on top of it as he walked into my office for our sessions. While he originally booked in to see me to help him with treating his crippling anxiety, our sessions together became more about lessons on finding himself. Like many young males, most of his life happened behind his bedroom door while studying, reading and watching adult animated series—the ones with a surprisingly sharp, intellectual edge that sometimes went over my head. 'You've got to watch *BoJack Horseman*', he'd always remind me, obviously recommending it to me because there was something about it he thought I would find interesting (and yes, I did find it interesting, and yes, I think some of it went over my head). At home, Brent only surfaced for feeding and watering, weaving around the house to avoid eye contact with his parents—not because he didn't like them, but because he couldn't be bothered engaging in lengthy but very normal parentally inquisitive conversations with them.

Among our chats about what was going on in his life, including him studying to become a lawyer, much of the conversation revolved around relationships, or the lack thereof. Brent had been single far longer than he would have liked, after breaking up with his long-time partner the year prior. Prior to that he'd had what he described as a 'messy few years' of short-term relationships and flings, with men and women, during which he was trying to figure out who he was—trying on different identities and personas to see what felt right for him. He thought he had figured out who he was and found the 'perfect guy', so he had settled into that relationship for a few years. When that didn't work out, he felt disillusioned. He was confused and felt he really didn't know who he was at all.

As an introvert who much preferred books to parties, he rarely ventured out and was reluctant to meet new people. Although well supported by his family and close friends, he still felt a hesitancy with new people. He wasn't confident in being authentically himself unless he felt comfortable and safe with a new person. He was still settling into his sexuality, but there were other parts of him that he also kept to himself—things he thought of as different or against the grain of what most of the population deemed normal. Like many young people, who have been fed a bunch of lies from the social media hive, he didn't really feel like he belonged and felt quite out of alignment with what he felt society wanted. Over time, the isolation left him feeling lonely and increasingly anxious, and then his father was diagnosed with cancer. Anxiety loves spare time, and it has no trouble finding you when you're holed up in your room alone while going through something traumatic. It loves it even more when you didn't feel comfortable with yourself in the first place.

There were a few different reasons we could hypothesise as being behind the increase in anxiety. Brent and I thoroughly discussed many of these, fleshing them out in each session, trying a host of techniques to help lessen his anxiety. We could see in each session how much progress he was making. As anyone who's experienced anxiety before, reducing it can make such a difference to your wellbeing. 'These sessions have changed my life', he said one day, when we decided to push our weekly sessions out to a six-week check-in, as his anxiety was diminishing and he was feeling happier and more settled.

But throughout our sessions together, there was something else that I had noticed in our conversations. Occasionally, when he house-sat for some friends who had a dog, he'd find himself outside more often—walking, moving and engaging with the world. Each time, he noticed a lift in his mood and anxiety, and he always reported that his week at their home had been so refreshing. It was not so much a social thing, but rather that he was moving … *outside* (with the bonus company of a doggo). There's nothing like a golden retriever staring at you to encourage you to get your sneakers on. I had suggested physical activity (and a dog) more times than I could count in our psychological consults, not only to ease loneliness but also as an extremely helpful tool to reduce anxiety, but he'd say it wasn't his thing, so he constantly brushed it off. Like many clients, it took him a while to take some advice on board, but when I pointed it out to him—the difference in his wellbeing in general while on his house-sitting weeks versus when he was living in his bedroom—he changed his mind. Over time, he started to incorporate more walks into his schedule, and one day, quite unexpectedly, he announced he'd joined a gym. His anxiety eased, his confidence grew and, funnily enough, I saw him less after that—just the occasional check-in. On our last session together, he reported that he'd met a new guy at the gym, another bookish, clever soul, and they've been together ever since. To quote from *War and Peace*, 'Everything comes in time to him who knows how to wait'. How apt.

One of the greatest gifts of being single is realising that you are a unique individual. Nature provided you with some innate traits when you were born (thanks to your parents), and your environment and experiences provided part of your story so far. It's nature and nurture. We are born with certain traits, but there is a complex interaction between them and the environment in which we live, culminating in our experience of life. This combination has amalgamated to make you the person you are today, and your individuality is what separates you from others. We try on different parts of people along the way—some of which sticks and some of which doesn't. We also put parts of our own true self down along the way, depending on the interactions we have with people on our life journey. Some of our interests, behaviours and even our traits may be sitting dormant inside of us, like unexplored potential. They're still inside of us but they have nowhere to go, particularly when we believe that the external world has no place for these parts. Life is happening all around us, and we adjust ourselves accordingly. No wonder so many of us are out of alignment, shapeshifting our way through life—no wonder it's sometimes nicer just being in our bedroom in our trackie dacks, hanging out and being our true selves.

One of the most important discussions I have with my clients is to get them to think about their 'self'—who they are, separate from everyone else. This involves thinking deeply about all their characteristics: their traits, behaviours, styles … everything and anything that they can think of that identifies them as their self. Usually, because they often start seeing me as a therapist for other reasons, people begin to think about their self by describing the way they are feeling, such as depressed, lonely, unfit, uncertain, shy or whatever else they perceive as contributing to how they are currently feeling and standing in their way as they try to move towards a better life. Almost like a 'protective self' that keeps controlling not only the show, but the rhetoric around the show. It's the self that you've unconsciously shaped through every experience, big and small—one that's always scanning for danger, always prioritising survival. Before you even have a chance to think, this part of you jumps in to shield, defend and manage the world on your behalf, often without your awareness. Sometimes when we identify these parts of us, and observe how they have taken control in previous relationships, it gives us a valuable 'aha' moment that we can apply to our life going forward. Some of my clients have realised that not only was their 'protective self' controlling their personal daily life, but it had been in control for their past relationships. They have noted how traits like perfectionism, jealousy, passivity (in relationships), unhealthiness, negativity and cynicism come up time and time again. These are traits that we don't want to have and yet seem to be there regardless, dominating and driving our behaviours, often unconsciously. I think we can all look back at previous relationships and identify certain traits of our own that weren't particularly helpful at the time. It's such a helpful reflection to have and can really shine a light on what we want for our self and our possible relationships in the future.

Instead of sitting in the 'protective self' chat for too long, I quickly turn towards discussing my clients' 'true self' with them—getting them to think about all their best traits, the ones that truly feel like them and are real and authentic. Imagine how you feel when you're wearing the right clothes that fit perfectly. You feel so good when you're wearing them. It's that kind of feeling —real and true to you.

When my clients do this exercise, reflecting on their positive traits, they come up with a whole host of characteristics: kind to others, trusting, warm, healthy, brave, creative, honest and even content. I then ask them, who has been controlling you for far too long? Is it your 'protective self'—the one that is causing the discontent? Often, it has been … for far too long.

The interesting thing about identifying the qualities of our protective selves is that we are discovering something deep about ourselves. This understanding gives us clarity about what we know we don't want to be like, and what is an opportunity for growth for us. If we've identified that our 'protective self' is depressed, lonely, unfit, uncertain and shy, then that's a valuable insight. If we flip these words to happy, connected, fit, certain and confident, and tag them on to the end of our 'true self' list, then we have more clarity about where our true self needs to take control, where we may need to do a little work and if we need more support to make it happen.

We want to get to the place where the best version of us is controlling our life—not the 'protective self', which may be trying to protect us because of the experiences we've had in the past. Our 'true self' is the wiser part of us and, while still imperfect, it seeks to continue to learn and grow by making intentional choices. Once we look at our 'true self' list, we need to think about what actions or what behaviours we need to take to actualise these traits. What small step do you need to take to be happier today? What action can you take, even for 20 minutes a day, to feel fitter? What little behaviour do you have to change to feel confident, even if just for a moment? Our 'true self' guides us to slowly become better than we were before, using all the wisdom we've gained from our experiences.

It's about aligning our mindset, rituals and habits with the most positive and real version of ourselves. The French writer and mathematician Blaise Pascal wisely said: 'All of humanity's problems stem from man's inability to sit quietly in a room alone'. Imagine what we could conjure up and become if we spent more time on our 'selves'. We would find the freedom to step more into what we want to be and work more on what we don't want to be.

Our true self needs intention, patience and practice, and most of all it needs time alone to actualise these needs.

Motto

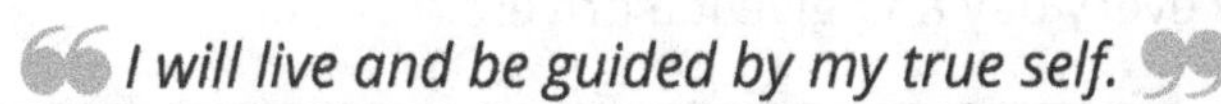

I will live and be guided by my true self.

Challenge: Discover Your True Self

Sometimes our protective self — along with some of its unhelpful traits — takes control of our life, without our awareness. We truly want to operate differently but, like many of our unconscious habits, sometimes they just take over automatically, even when in our conscious world they are not working for us anymore. This takes a little work, and some active work!

Write a list of at least 10 positive traits or attributes about yourself. This could be anything from fun, loyal and hardworking through to stylish (go you!). Write a heading on top of that list and call it 'My True Self'. Then, write down some of the traits or attributes you have that, with some reflection, you find a little challenging or could be areas of growth for you. With this second list, flip those more negative words to something opposite or positive. For example, you might have written 'low self-esteem', so you can change that to 'confident'. You might have written 'exhausted', so you can change that to 'energised'. You might have written 'lonely', so you can change that to 'connected'. Add those new, more positive words to your 'My True Self' list. What a fabulous list you will have!

Next, think of some activities you can do on a reasonably regular basis to make sure that these traits and attributes are lit up. It might mean consciously taking the time to relax more, or even taking up a new physical activity to energise you! Your 'true self' needs to take the steering wheel of your life, so pick a new activity every day and give it a drive!

Chapter 20

Alone Too Long

I'm going to let you in on a little secret. I'm a bit obsessed with books on manifestation. I just can't get enough of them. My bookshelves are lined with the works of spiritual teachers and modern gurus, from books written by authors studying the ancient wisdom of sages and shamans to those written using evidence-based neuroscience—and yes, even the more 'woo-woo' takes on manifesting. I've spent countless hours soaking up the teachings, the lessons and the techniques. In fact, in the most challenging moments I've gone through in my adult life, counterintuitively (or come to think of it, intuitively), I've reached for manifesting books over other self-help books. I just love them, and I often re-read them to remind me of their wisdom, particularly when life gets tricky. They've given me hope, a sense of control and a feeling of joy that my dreams may come to fruition, perhaps with a sprinkle of magic, and that something bigger than me may be able to help me along the way. Over the years, many of the people I've worked with have said the same thing: these books kept them feeling positive, even when life didn't.

But one of the biggest mistakes I see people make when trying to manifest something is that they become obsessed with *that one thing*, believing it's the ultimate key to their happiness, the solution to everything that feels off in their life. It's usually the thing they feel is lacking in the present moment. A 'lack of' mentality has left them feeling without, upset and sometimes a little panicky, and this way of thinking is often what has led them to read these books in the first place. I'd even go as far as to say they are emotionally driven to find out how they can quickly fix their life to get out of the distressed state that they are in. For some people, they want more money. For others, they think they need a new job, a beautiful home or better health. And rightly so! Many of us are having challenging times with all these areas of our life. But for far too many of us, the thing people seem to think they need to fix their life is to find the 'perfect' partner. The 'one'. The person that will solve all their problems, and all the world's ills. They spend hours visualising, writing manifesting lists and doing all the rituals they've been told will make it happen. They need to be good-looking, fit, healthy, successful and loving, all in the one package, as though throwing all those things in a cauldron with an eye of newt is going to actualise them. And then—and only then—will they be happy. They focus so much on *getting* that one person that they forget to live the rest of their life.

Manifesting books tell us to put our intentions out there: imagine that person and what your relationship will be like, act as if it's happening now, and feel that inside of you. We use all our senses to become that future version of ourselves who's already in love, and we get swept up in the hope and excitement of manifesting that perfect person. But here's the missing link, the part so many readers overlook (even though it's plain as day): *you must get on with your life*. You must start being your most content self now, not sit around waiting for someone else to show up. A partner isn't the end goal that leads to happiness. Happiness comes from all the parts of our lives—it's the cumulative effect of everything that leads to the good stuff, not just one part of our lives.

It's all well and good to talk about the benefits of being alone, but many people deeply desire a partner. In their estimation, they have been by themselves for far too long. They still feel that something is missing. Regardless, you have one life to live, and it's far better to get on with living it than to sit and wait. What if the 'right person' never shows up, and you've spent years putting your life on pause in the meantime? Bring yourself back to the present. Be more *you*. Don't while away your days waiting for someone to arrive. Instead, focus on becoming the best version of you. The version that doesn't want to wait but wants to live fully *now*. If you are feeling that something is missing, ask yourself: is it really another person? Or is something else missing in your life that is making you not feel whole? The real work isn't in the searching for the missing piece of the puzzle, it's in becoming complete yourself.

Our wellbeing tends to be stronger when we spread our 'eggs' across many baskets in life, rather than placing them all in one. It's rarely healthy to invest our entire sense of self in a single area, and yet time and time again I see people pour everything into the *relationship* basket. When that relationship breaks down, they often attach their entire sense of worth to it, so when it disappears, their self-worth crumbles with it. But those who nurture a variety of areas in their life—friendships, interests, career, health, creativity, community—tend to cope far better when one part falters. It's a bit like being a workaholic: if work is all you have, losing your job can feel like losing your identity. But if you've cultivated the other parts of yourself, you soften the blow.

The same applies to relationships. If you haven't yet found a partner but you're investing in the rest of your life—you're feeling whole, well and content within yourself—then it may be a good time to open yourself up to meeting someone. Schedule time to connect with new people. Do all the things we've been talking about in this book. The difference is that this time, you're searching from a place of wholeness rather than need. You'll be more attuned to how you feel around others, more aware of what lifts you up and what doesn't, and more likely to spot red flags early — and so you'll quickly ditch the people that are not right for you, or who give you the creeps. You might even find yourself a little fussier than you used to be, and that's a very good thing (it takes one to know one).

How long is 'too long' to be alone? Of course, it's subjective. For some, a few days without a partner feels unbearable. For others, a few months is too much. And then there are those who have been on their own for years and feel perfectly content. (I should actually win the prize for this one.)

Personally, I'm tall enough to reach the high shelves, strong enough to wrestle open a tight jam jar and capable of looking after myself in almost every way. Sure, I wouldn't mind someone to fill my car with petrol. Though with a new electric car on the horizon, even that will soon be a moot point. The truth is, I don't *need* anyone for anything; anyone who comes into my life will simply be a wonderful bonus to the life I already have. And it's only from a point of wholeness that you can say that.

Live your fullest life while you are alone … you will find yourself.

Motto

Challenge: Living a Life That's Not on Hold

Sometimes when we're alone but we are waiting for that perfect person to materialise, we can accidentally put our life on hold. Most of us don't even like sitting on hold on the telephone, yet we do it in our life for a variety of reasons. It's a very understandable feeling, and one that tends to come with a host of negative emotions, including sadness, frustration and stress. This in turn causes us to press pause on many of the things we desire in life. But every moment between when you are (or your life is) placed on hold and when you are (or your life is) taken off hold is sacred. Every moment is important. Every moment is your life.

Think of the many activities that you would love to do which you may have been waiting to do with a partner. They might be large or small, but you know that you have pressed pause on them. It could be something like travelling, working interstate, or even going to a fancy restaurant or on a weekend away. Write a list of them. Try and prioritise, from the easiest to do through to the hardest. Yes, sometimes you will have to rally the troops and get your mates on board, but these are the fun activities that you will enjoy and it's important that you achieve them! Try 'unpausing' your life and tackle one each month.

Chapter 21

Not Lonely and Not Alone

You know those 'Rules of the House' signs that people put up as decorative boards in their homes? You might find them hanging in the kitchen or the family room, as a little reminder (and sometimes a gentle warning) of the expectations about how everyone in the household should treat one another. Common decrees might be a pleasant 'Always say please and thank you', a wise 'Laugh often' or a psychologically helpful, 'Forgive quickly'. I have a polite rectangular canvas version of this hung on the wall in my hallway, listing in different-sized fonts some common rules for our house and for just being a reasonably decent human being. Mind you, I don't think anyone who lives in my house has ever stopped to read it, despite them walking by it thousands of times. When I hear some of the 'verbal exchanges' in the kitchen and the bathroom in the mornings, it seems some of the messages, like 'Be kind always' and 'Care for others', have been selectively attended to by my teenagers, as clearly they have not chosen to apply these rules to each other. I hope they've at least been subliminally absorbing some of these messages over the years, so they can apply them once they launch into the adult world.

But whether overtly hung on the wall of the home or not, many groups of human beings who live together have certain rules they follow. Whether the home houses a family with children or a group of students or mates, there need to be some common directives so that everyone is in some sort of alignment. These rules are usually there to keep everyone on the same page; what's good for the group is good for everyone. The rules exist to maintain harmony, prevent chaos and nudge people back into line if their actions start causing friction. It's the same idea in society at large: rules and regulations help govern behaviour, protect the group and keep things running smoothly. Without them, life would be messy, unpredictable and often stressful. For everyone.

But here's the thing: what's best for the group isn't always what's best for the individual in terms of our own personal fulfilment. A lot of us grow up absorbing the values of our culture, our parents and our immediate family. For years, sometimes decades, we live as if these beliefs are our own. We follow the rules, adopt the habits and assume we think what we think because it feels right, when, really, we've just inherited these things. It's only when we step away, leave home or create space for ourselves that we begin to question: 'Do I believe this? Do I want this? Is this really me?' Sometimes, that realisation can hit like a bolt of lightning: we've been living according to someone else's blueprint, not our own. It can take time to figure out who you truly are, what you value, what excites you, what you reject and what you want from life. It can feel like a slow unfolding, or a sudden epiphany. Either way, it's the start of living in alignment with yourself, not just following the rules of the collective.

The chance to have some time alone can separate you from people a little and give you chance to live by your own rules. You can create a little world of your own for a while, and you can follow your own rules however you please. You have the freedom and the opportunity to live by and test your own rules for life (however absurd) without having to worry about accommodating anyone. No compromises, no argy-bargy with someone else's beliefs and no negotiating according to someone else's values. If I think about my ideal rules for life, they may not be sustainable when living with other people (and perhaps they are the reason why I'm still single).

For example, mine look like this:

> Don't lie
> Most meetings should be emails
> Animals are friends, not food
> Only go to the cinema to watch a movie if Tom Cruise is in it
> You probably don't have to go to that event
> Never go to a shopping centre on a Saturday
> Pets are allowed on the bed and can do whatever they want
> Bedtime is 9 pm or earlier
> Reverse parking in carparks should be banned
> Don't mansplain to me
> You can say it quieter
> If I must line up, I'm not buying it/going there/waiting for it
> It's fine to have lots of cats

Of course, most of these things are not followed, but I'd like them to be.

Everyone's rules would be different—that's the point. Alone, you get the chance to notice what really matters to you, live according to your own quirks and values, and maybe even enjoy the little freedoms that come from being unapologetically yourself. You can do *more of this* when you have time alone. This is a good thing.

Many people will live with people their whole lives and may never get the chance to feel lonely. They may feel quite content in their group, in their family and with their connections. But it certainly doesn't mean that having some alone time now and again wouldn't benefit them. Consider these catch-cries of modern-day adults—words and phrases I've heard so many times from clients over the years in times of stress, overwhelm, busy-ness and pressure, most of which are in response to being healthily (and unhealthily) connected to others: 'I just want some time myself!', 'I just want some peace!', 'I need some me-time', 'I can't even think straight', 'I just want to go the toilet *alone*'. Inevitably, even when we are with other people and connected to them, we're not always our best selves either.

For couples, some alone time in the waking hours may benefit them, but so might some alone time while they're sleeping. A 'sleep divorce' involves couples choosing to sleep in separate beds or bedrooms regularly, to get a better night's sleep. Like many 'newly' discovered internet fads, sleeping in separate bedrooms isn't new. Most people can recall childhood visits to the grandparents, peeking into every room and noticing that grandma and grandpa sleep in different beds, or even separate rooms entirely. People in relationships have been sleeping separately forever (truth be told) but, lately, sleep separation arrangements are gaining popularity, with millennials reportedly leading the trend by opting to sleep in separate rooms from their partners (something that older generations seem to have considered a little too shameful to share). With an ever-increasing consciousness about what's important for our mental and physical health, younger generations are more educated in knowing what's good for them, and with that knowledge they are speaking out about the importance of getting a healthy amount of sleep. They're also more serious about putting necessary health-promoting measures in place, even if that means their loved one gets to count sheep at the other end of the house. The decision to sleep separately may stem from differences in sleep schedules, incompatible sleep habits or a need for different sleeping environments (too hot, too cold, too much noise, too quiet, and so on). Some people also have a greater need for personal space during the night, while some parents must share their personal space with a small child to get some shut-eye, taking turns with their partner so they each have a night off. For those who choose a sleep separation, it might be temporary while they navigate a certain period in their lives; for some other couples, they've found it the best way forward for their relationship. While the term 'divorce' may suggest negative connotations, a sleep divorce may prevent a real divorce by allowing people to create their optimal sleep environments. At the very least, people save on ear plugs, eye masks and the time taken to elbow their partners in the ribs for snoring. But perhaps there are many other areas in a couple's life that would benefit from time alone.

Some people are not lonely at all, nor are they alone, *but* they are still experiencing the distress of not having moments to themselves. Too much of anything is a bad thing … right? Divorce sounds a bit harsh, but a temporary 'separation of activities' might do people some good. Whether that means separate socialising, exercising, hobbies or holidays, it gives each person in a couple time to reap the benefits: time to individually feel, think, create, reflect and be. We need to find the Goldilocks position of aloneness — enough time to 'be' by our 'selves' but also enough time doing all the things that our 'selves' need to function at our best. Given what we've talked about throughout the book, think about the multitude of benefits of some alone time for different people in different situations: a young stay-at-home mum who has been looking after her kids at home all day; an elderly man who has been caring for his wife at home all day; parents having separate time with their friends on the weekend now and again while the other parent looks after the kids. Think of how much better they would be at fulfilling any role in life, whether parenting, caring or otherwise, if they had the time to nurture other meaningful areas of their life. A chance for some downtime, a chance to reflect and a chance to look after themselves can help them be a better version of themselves when they return to each their partner after some alone time.

How can we use the learnings of being alone so that we can incorporate more 'alone' time in our lives, even when we are surrounded by people, have a partner and don't feel lonely? The benefits don't have to be gained from long periods of solitude. They can arise through giving ourselves a few regular moments of time to ourselves—a weekend away with the girls, a hotel stay for one, a hike with the dog, a golf game with mates, more time for taking career opportunities or an interruption-free afternoon with a book.

We need these little moments of aloneness—a moment to reset and recharge that tops up what the self needs, so we can be a better version of ourselves for others.

Motto

> 66 *I will put the oxygen mask on first and ritualise moments of 'alone' for my own wellbeing.* 99

Challenge: Ritualising Some Alone Time

Whether you are surrounded by people or not, there are many benefits to having some time to yourself. It gives you time to relax, recharge, re-energise and reset, all in your own company.

For people that are constantly with others, it can be hard to separate yourself from them, physically and psychologically, so it is crucial to retain a sense of self and to ritualise some moments alone. Reflect on whether you do, indeed, have enough time to yourself. Be honest with yourself here — does the thought of reading a book alone, taking an afternoon walk in nature, watching a movie by yourself, having a night out at a book club meeting or taking yourself away for a night in a hotel sound blissful? If it does, there's a high chance you're not getting enough alone time! Have a think: if some time alone is feasible, book it in your schedule and communicate to your partner that you are taking some time to yourself, even if it's just for 30 minutes. After a month of doing this weekly, notice how you feel.

Epilogue

Recently, I had the most intense dream I've probably ever had in my life.

I know most of us have strange dreams while we are sleeping, many of which, upon awakening, we declare as being slightly weird—teeth falling out, standing naked in front of a crowd, being chased by a gigantic T-Rex wearing a builder's hat and holding a piece of cheese, whose face happens to be the same as a girl from school…the usual dream content. Our inner armchair dream expert self-analyses to make sense of these nonsensical occurrences.

Often, perhaps within seconds, we forget these dreams, the brain deeming them unimportant and not worthy of even pushing them to our short-term memory so we can at least tap into the meaning of them. It would be good to have some time to learn from these dreams, seeing as we've spent so much time entertaining them in our sleep!

However, a few dreams do pass through. We get to think about them for a few minutes before they slowly dissipate out of the mind, as quickly as the new thoughts of the day enter. We lose the interesting movie-like sequences and contents of our dreams, as well as the powerful messages that went with them. So, I find it intriguing that I'm *still* thinking about my extraordinary dream now. There must be a reason why my mind has deemed it to be remember-worthy.

I noted it all down straight away in my little notebook in my bedroom drawer, labelling it the 'Kevin Costner dream'.

The dream is quite hard to explain. Yes, Kevin Costner was in the dream, but that wasn't the most intense part of it (although, perhaps if the dream went in a different direction, it could have been—maybe next time). It wasn't the setting that made it so interesting either, and there weren't even any words exchanged in the dream; instead, it was the concoction of feelings that I (the dreamer) experienced while in the dream that lingered for hours afterwards.

The famous neurologist and founder of psychoanalysis, Sigmund Freud, believed that dreams had two types of content: the manifest content, which is the literal subject matter of the dream, and the latent content, which is the underlying meaning of the symbols in the subject matter. *My* dream wasn't technically *about* Kevin Costner—it was about what he represented. Kevin Costner was the subject (the *manifest content*) of my dream, while the underlying meaning (the *latent content*) was something that has stayed with me ever since.

In the dream sequence, Kevin Costner was kitted out in a black-and-white tuxedo and bow tie, with his hair slicked back (which, even while dreaming, also kind of felt like a false memory that my mind had implanted from a movie I'd watched him in). I know I was wearing a dress, but I couldn't begin to describe it to you because my eyes were on Kevin. We were mingling with other people, all of whom I didn't know, perhaps on a boat or at some sort of social event. I had a sense that this event was about me—many of the people knew me and were intentionally heading in my direction to talk to me. Kevin was my partner, my plus one, and he was holding my hand as we mingled with these people with ease. But the dream wasn't really about the event, or what we were doing—nor did it revolve around what Kevin looked like (although he was looking mighty fine). It was about the feeling that hit me in that moment—the sensation of being in that type of loving relationship. The feeling itself was powerful: being loved, adored, valued, cherished…— feeling like I truly mattered to someone. This person was simply there for me. It was the kind of feeling I don't think I've had for decades—the kind that sweeps through you when you first fall in love or know that someone is 'in love' with you. It was familiar. It's that mix of desire and devotion, when you're not just lustful but also adoring, or being adored. When you know someone is listening to you closely, hanging on to every word, as if nothing else matters. It's that feeling when you know that person totally, one hundred per cent has your back. I had felt that way before, maybe for a little while, *but* it was such a distant memory.

To me, the Kevin Costner dream wasn't just a dream; it was a memory and a reminder of what is possible. It was such a strong feeling, so potent, that to this day I'm still rattled by it. But I'm rattled in a good way. It may seem a little perfect, maybe a little movie-like, but it strangely came into my dreams at the most perfect of times. On a spiritual level, the way that dream entered my mind felt like the universe, my spirit or even my soul was reminding me that this was a feeling I needed to experience again in my lifetime—but most importantly, it was reminding me that I should never settle for anything less. It was like someone commanding me from above (or within) in a Morgan Freeman-like voice 'Thou shalt not settle for anything less', followed by a swift, 'In the meantime, get on with it girl', It felt like a message for me to get comfortable with waiting a little longer for the things I really deserve.

Even though I have not been in a relationship for quite a while and I feel content in my life, it doesn't mean there aren't moments when I think I *should* be a little more open to meeting a special someone and having them in my life. Perhaps I do need to be a bit more proactive. I might feel this way when I see a post on social media about a new celebrity couple who have finally met 'the one'; I might see some photos on Facebook of old friends who've been together forever on their latest camping trip with their family and feel a pang; I might watch a movie about two people who fall in love and wonder about my own romantic future. Yet when I reflect more deeply, I can see that many of those moments are not shaped by me. They are shaped by an external pull, the quiet insistence of society that says I *should* be in a relationship—that being alone is somehow not enough.

Maybe we were paying attention to the wrong message in some of those Disney movies we watched as kids. Maybe it wasn't really about princesses finding true love. Maybe the real lesson was 'Don't bother the witches in the forest'. They weren't evil; they were just grumpy because they were perfectly content in their cosy cottages alone, probably in the middle of a really good book. Leave them be.

I don't want to sugar-coat being alone either. At times, it's bloody hard. Whether you feel like you don't have enough to do to keep you busy, or whether you have too much to do because you're overloaded with too many tasks to tackle by yourself, it's important to acknowledge that it can be challenging to be alone. Hold space for it. I've had moments where I've been literally knee-deep in a). problems, b). bills, c). sewerage, d). all of the above (the answer is d), and I've thought how much easier it would be if I could share this with someone—emotionally and practically. And there have been times when I wouldn't have minded being able to share something exciting that's happening in my life with someone else. It *can* be wonderful to have someone special to share both the good and the bad. But again, it's the *idea* of that someone I am thinking of—and perhaps the reality might not be so wonderful. And going back to 'all of the above', I figured it out on my own anyway (with a little help from my village ... and a good plumber). I could do it then. And I can do it again if I need to. Alone.

From working with hundreds of people over the years, what I know for sure is that there are far too many people who feel unhappy in their romantic relationships. There are too many people whose lives are on hold until they find a partner; too many people who are caught in repeating patterns; too many people who are searching for themselves in someone else; too many people trying to fix their loneliness by filling it with the wrong people or unhealthy things, rather than understanding what those feelings are really telling them. All the while, they are not entertaining the space in between relationships that can bring so many unexpected gifts.

There's something wonderful about being middle-aged and by yourself. I'm not sure if it's because I'm getting older and a little grumpier, but I think part of it comes from having spent decades doing 'the right thing'. So much of my life has been spent doing things for other people — people-pleasing, being compliant, being nice, putting on a façade and saying yes when I really wanted to say no. Looking back, my life seems to have moved so quickly that I feel as though I've never truly had the chance to live exactly how I want to — to shape a day exactly as I would like it to look, free from the pressures that have weighed on my shoulders for far too long. In my twenties, I was happy going with the flow, moving along the socially defined pathway I'd been placed on, never really questioning if I should have chosen another route: one less worn, one less obvious. Back then, I hadn't even considered the road less travelled.

My children are older now, stepping into their late teenage years. With their growing independence, there's less of a constant demand on me. For the first time in a long time, I'm not rushing to give away my energy or my presence. Instead, I'm savouring the silence, the space, the small moments that ask nothing of me other than to simply be. And I'm enjoying it, so much so that I look at my calendar—the tasks, the work, the duties, the roles and the hats I wear—and I ask myself, 'What I can I give up? What can I stop doing? What can I give away? What can I say no to? What can I press pause on? What can I cancel?' All in the name of spending more time alone, so I can savour that time and do more of the things that my soul calls for. While most people might assume that eventually I'll grow restless and want to put myself back out there (as society would totally deem my relationship gap years as being socially unacceptable), what I've discovered is quite the opposite. Rather than craving companionship, I find myself craving more solitude. It's almost like solitude has become beautifully addictive to me. I need more alone time. I realise that I need much more time alone than I'd previously been allowing myself.

Maybe you do too, and you haven't quite realised this … yet.

101 Lovely Things to Do When You're Alone

Courtesy of my friends, family and clients over the years (with many thrown in from myself, of course)

This is a handy cheat sheet you can refer to forever. Whenever you find yourself feeling lonely, whether it be for a brief moment or for a while, you can peruse this rather long list to spark some inspiration. Some of these activities you can do totally alone, in your own home, or even out in your community. For other activities, you might like to take your (or someone else's) furry friend along for the journey. A by-product of many of these activities is that you are likely to not only connect with yourself more, but also other people. So, scroll through the list and pick an activity that most excites you!

1. Learn an instrument
2. Watch a good movie that you know you have enjoyed in the past
3. Join an art class
4. Tend your garden

5. Go on a hike to the local forest/bush
6. Get nostalgic and look through old photo albums
7. Go to a concert
8. Take up a new sport
9. Listen to a podcast (there are millions of them!)
10. Buy some paints and start painting
11. Create a new recipe and play with new flavours
12. Sleep—a full takeover of the bed, with no obstructions
13. Have a long shower with all your special scrubs
14. Watch a sunrise
15. Pat some cats
16. Plant a vegetable garden
17. Go waterfall hunting in the hills
18. Spend some time at your local café, drinking coffee
19. Go for a long (or short) walk
20. Do some yoga at home or join a local yoga class
21. Visit an elderly person and have a chat to them (they are *very* interesting)
22. Head to a day spa
23. Go and get a massage
24. See a movie at the cinema and enjoy all the popcorn yourself
25. Make a nice meal or snack for yourself
26. Watch a documentary to learn something new
27. Try on outrageously expensive clothes in a store that you have no intention of buying
28. Wander around cute shops
29. Go to the beach—and go to a different one each time you go
30. Organise a night out with your mates
31. Take a bubble bath and put some candles on
32. Dust off some old records and play them

33. Watch a sunset
34. Put the windows up in the car, with your favourite songs blaring, and sing like nobody is watching
35. Take an opportunity in your career
36. Have a nap during the day
37. Volunteer at a local community garden
38. Sing along to your favourite songs (or join a local choir)
39. Clean out one room of your house
40. Look up at the stars
41. Go to a beautiful park in your town (and change it up each week)
42. Start knitting
43. Go window shopping
44. Drive in your car, look at random scenery and just get lost
45. Go out with your mates for the evening specifically to dance
46. Go travelling in your state
47. Cook for people less fortunate
48. Sign up for a new course online
49. Head to the zoo and wander around
50. Phone a friend to have a chat
51. Chill with a wine (or the drink of your choice) in a trendy bar
52. Journal more and start writing your memoir
53. Have a pamper hour with face masks, lotions and potions
54. Join a birdwatching club
55. Head to a new bakery in your town and try it out
56. Swim at the local pool
57. Go away for the weekend to a remote town
58. Paint a picture
59. Decorate your house
60. Write a letter to someone

61. Join a charity or do some volunteer work
62. Take a dog on a walk or hike (if the dog is high energy)
63. Go to a matinee at the theatre
64. Do some exercise—put on some tunes and get sweaty
65. Wander around your local library
66. Start to learn a new language
67. Chill at the beach and read a book
68. Play a round of golf (or mini golf)
69. Wander through a museum
70. Go to a local market
71. Join a lobby group for a cause you are passionate about
72. Try some adventure sports
73. Drive a long distance and see what you find
74. Organise a mates' weekend
75. While away the time with a good magazine
76. Volunteer at a local animal shelter
77. Find your old nineties CDs and have some friends over
78. Walk a dog on a slow Sniffari (purely for the scent enjoyment—it's amazing what dogs will notice!)
79. Think about an overseas holiday and start planning it
80. Join a local book club
81. Take yourself off to a shopping centre that you don't normally go to
82. Learn to make a new cuisine, perhaps via a cooking class
83. Soak your feet and give yourself a foot spa
84. Get out some jigsaw puzzles
85. Go to a dance class in your town
86. Hang out in your front garden and talk to passers-by
87. Go visit all the antique shops in your city
88. Start a new business side hustle
89. Learn photography
90. Look for pictures in the clouds—use your imagination!

91. Join an improv class to improve your confidence—and
    to have fun!
92. Learn to be a better public speaker
93. Track down the perfect vintage outfit
94. Go to a farmers' market to find organic ingredients for
    your next recipe
95. Do some meditation
96. Rearrange your furniture
97. Bake some delicious biscuits or cakes
98. Laze on the couch with a face mask
99. Help someone out that is doing it tougher than you
100. Get a new qualification online
101. Alright…*go on a date*

The *Only You* Monthly Review

This review is a monthly self-reflection tool to
help you invest in your life.

Part III of this book helps you get comfortable with *being only you* so you can tap into who you truly are. It's about all the little things you can do to be proactive in looking after your self, and being the best version of you. Chapters 11–19 provide specific areas you can reflect on over time, which is where this monthly review comes in.

At the end of each month, reflect on each of the *Only You* segments in Chapters 11–19 that show the different areas of your life that need to be nurtured so you can be the best version of you. Don't worry about being too exact—this is a reflective exercise to get you thinking honestly about where your strengths are, and where there are opportunities for growth for you. There are only so many hours in the day, so this simple exercise is designed to get you thinking about where you were this past month, and where you would like to head in the next month.

Imagine yourself as a vessel of light, divided into nine smaller compartments. Each compartment holds your energy for a different area of life. Notice which compartments are glowing brightly and which ones are dim. The goal is to consciously rebalance your life so you can shine as your most aligned and true self. Start thinking about where to direct your light in the coming month, and what actions can help each compartment glow a little brighter.

1. Relish in Your Presence

Ask: How bright is the light in this compartment?

Action: What will I do this month to improve this area of my life?

2. Follow Your Inner Compass

Ask: How bright is the light in this compartment?

Action: What will I do this month to improve this area of my life?

3. Master Your Mind

Ask: How bright is the light in this compartment?

Action: What will I do this month to improve this area of my life?

4. Listen to Your Emotions

Ask: How bright is the light in this compartment?

Action: What will I do this month to improve this area of my life?

5. Own Your Inner Strength

Ask: How bright is the light in this compartment?

Action: What will I do this month to improve this area of my life?

6. Tap into Your Creativity

Ask: How bright is the light in this compartment?

Action: What will I do this month to improve this area of my life?

7. Nurture Your Relationships

Ask: How bright is the light in this compartment?

Action: What will I do this month to improve this area of my life?

8. Self-Compassion for Your Lonely

Ask: How bright is the light in this compartment?

Action: What will I do this month to improve this area of my life?

9. Discover Your True Self

Ask: How bright is the light in this compartment?

Action: What will I do this month to improve this area of my life?

References

Chapter 1: Feeling Lonely

Hari, J, 2018. *Lost Connections*. Bloomsbury USA.

Wilde, O, 1890. *The Picture of Dorian Gray*. Lippincott's Monthly Magazine.

Chapter 2: The Trouble with Loneliness

World Health Organization, 2025. *From Loneliness to Social Connection—Charting a Path to Healthier Societies*.

Kent, EM *et al*, 2025. Loneliness is associated with decreased support and increased strain given in social relationships. *Psychophysiology*, vol. 62 (7), e70105.

Lazuras, L, Ypsilanti, A & Mullings, E, 2024. The emotional burden of loneliness and its association with mental health outcomes. *International Journal of Behavioural Medicine*, vol. 31 (3), pp. 372–379.

Shen, C *et al*, 2025. Plasma proteomic signatures of social isolation and loneliness associated with morbidity and mortality. *Nature Human Behaviour*, vol. 9, pp. 569–583.

Fitch, J, 2000. *White Oleander: A Novel*. Back Bay Books.

Chapter 5: Solitude Can Save You

Kaminski, R, 2025. *The Gift of Not Belonging*. Scribe.

McConaughey, M, 2020. *Greenlights*. Crown.

Lishman, M, 2024. *Crisis to Contentment: The Getting of Wisdom*, Mid-Life. Affirm Press.

Rodriguez, M, Schertz, KE & Kross, E, 2025. How people think about being alone shapes their experience of loneliness. *Nature Communications*, vol. 16, 1594.

Chapter 7: Sitting with a Broken Heart

Prasad, A, *et al*, 2008. Apical ballooning syndrome (Tako-Tsubo or stress cardiomyopathy): A mimic of acute myocardial infarction. *American Heart Journal*, vol. 155 (3), pp. 408–17.

Chapter 11: Relish in Your Presence

Beck, M, 2013. *Finding Your Way in a Wild New World: Reclaim Your True Nature to Create the Life You Want*. Atria Books.

Chapter 12: Follow Your Inner Compass

Livingstone, K, 15th September 1999. Anti-social, Antipodean and living next door to me. *The Independent*.

Chapter 13: Master Your Mind

Hittner, JB & Widholm, CD, 2024. Meta-analysis of the association between gratitude and loneliness. *Applied Psychology: Health & Well-Being*, vol. 16 (4), pp. 2520–2535.

Chapter 17: Nurture Your Relationships

Harvard Study of Adult Development. adultdevelopmentstudy.org.
Waldinger, R & Schulz, M, 19 January 2023. What the longest study on human happiness found is the key to a good life. *The Atlantic*.
Waldinger, R, 2015. *What makes a good life? Lessons from the longest study on happiness*. TEDx. ted.com/talks/robert_waldinger_what_makes_a_good_life_lessons_from_the_longest_study_on_happiness.
Sarkisian, N & Gerstel, N, 2015. Does singlehood isolate or integrate? Examining the link between marital status and ties to kin, friends, and neighbors. *Journal of Social and Personal Relationships*, vol. 33 (3), pp. 361–384.
Musick, K & Bumpass, L, 2012. Re-examining the case for marriage: Union formation and changes in well-being. *Journal of Marriage and Family*, vol. 74 (1), pp. 1–18.

Chapter 18: Self-Compassion for Your Lonely

Neff, K, 2023. Self-compassion: Theory, method, research, and intervention. *Annual Review of Psychology*, vol. 74, pp. 193–218.

Acknowledgements

Thank you to my agent, Simone Landes, who has helped me to actualise yet another book idea, one that I've been badgering her about for far too many years! Immense gratitude to my wonderful Wiley publishing team; Jordon Lott, Chris Shorten, Kerry Laundon, Ingrid Bond, and everybody else that worked so hard to bring this book to life and help me share it with readers around the world. This is a topic so close to my heart, and I know it will resonate with so many, so thank you for believing in it!

Thank you to my family and friends for their support and for listening to me waffle on about the next book I'm writing (I know, there's always at least one in my head). In particular, a big shoutout to my girl friends who I regularly share a wine, a dinner or a walk—all of whom have also tried to set me up with a guy at some point, and I fobbed them off probably way too quickly. Apologies for that. You can't rush these things!

And thank you, as always to my wonderful clients, past and present, who I have spent many an hour talking with—those who share their vulnerable stories with me, and teach me so much about life through the lens of others. It's been a privilege to work with you.

On the home front, my shiny kids, Lali and Luca—love you to infinity and beyond. And the fur babies who are always by my side, whether in real life, or just their fur stuck to my clothes … Chilly, Spooky, Biscoff (and of course, The Bird).